LAPTOPS AND MOBILE DEVICES
MADE EASY

Which? Books are commissioned and published by Which? Ltd,
2 Marylebone Road, London NW1 4DF
Email: books@which.co.uk

British Library Cataloguing in Publication Data
A catalogue record for this book is available from the British Library

Some of the material in this book has previously been published in Which?, in our Computing magazine and online

ISBN 978 1 84490 117 3

1 3 5 7 9 10 8 6 4 2

Acknowledgments: Microsoft product screen shot(s) used with permission from Microsoft Corporation. Microsoft, Encarta, MSN, and Windows are either registered trademarks or trademarks of Microsoft Corporation in the United States and/or other countries.

Apple products and product screen shots courtesy of Apple.

Picture credits: courtesy of Shutterstock: pages 8, 9, 11, 12, 14, 16, 17, 19, 20, 21, 23, 24 (top), 27–29, 44, 53, 59, 62, 64, 65, 66, 69, 71, 73, 74, 90, 125 (bottom), 133, 136, 137, 160–163, 170, 172, 175, 177, 179, 180, 183, 184, 208, 209, 211, 212; courtesy of Lynn Wright: pages 96, 98, 99, 105 (top, background), 111 (bottom), 114, 115, 166, 210

The publishers would like to thank Sarah Kidner, Matt Bath and the Which? Computing team for their help in the preparation of this book.

Consultant editor: Lynn Wright
Project manager: Julie Brooke
Designer: Blanche Williams, Harper-Williams
Proofreader: Carolyn Madden
Indexer: Diana Lecore
Printed and bound by Charterhouse, Hatfield
Distributed by Littlehampton Book Services Ltd, Faraday Close, Durrington, Worthing, West Sussex BN13 3RB

Essential Velvet is an elemental chlorine-free paper produced at Condat in Périgord, France using timber from sustainably managed forests. The mill is ISO14001 and EMAS certified.

For a full list of Which? Books, please call 01903 828557, access our website at www.which.co.uk, or write to Littlehampton Book Services. For other enquiries call 0800 252 100.

which?

LAPTOPS AND MOBILE DEVICES MADE EASY

▶ Contents

▶ LAPTOPS & NETBOOKS

Laptops and netbooks explained	8
Benefits of buying a laptop	10
Laptops tour	12
Netbooks tour	14
Ports	16
Processors	18
Memory and drives	20
Screen	22
Battery	24
Input devices	27
Graphics	28
Sound	29
Webcams	30
Networking features	33
Operating systems	34
Apple MacBooks explained	38
Deciding which laptop to buy	40
Buying a laptop: factors to bear in mind	43
Getting the best laptop deal	46
Setting up your laptop	48
Moving data from your old PC	52
Secure your laptop	56
Upgrading your laptop	59
Upgrading your laptop hard drive	63

▶ TABLET PCS

Tablet computers explained	68
Operating systems	70
Tablet features	72
Additional features	76
Apple iPad explained	78
Apple iPad operating system	82
Google Android tablet PCs explained	84
Android tablet operating system	86
Windows tablet PCs explained	88
Windows tablet PCs operating system	90
How to choose the right tablet for you	92
Setting up a tablet PC	96
Tablet applications	100
Tablet security	104

▶ EBOOK READERS

Ebooks and ebook readers explained	108
Ebook readers tour	110
Ebook reader features	112
Connectivity features	115
Choosing the right one for you	117
Setting up an ebook reader	119
Ebook formats	124
Ebook stores	125
Buy and download an ebook	126
Alternatives to ebook readers	129

▶ SMARTPHONES

Smartphones explained	132
Smartphones tour	134
Smartphone features	136
Smartphone batteries	138
Getting to grips with smartphone apps	140
Apple iPhone explained	142
Using the Apple iPhone App Store	144
Download an app from the iTunes Store	146
Essential iPhone tips	148
Android smartphones explained	150
Using the Android market	152
Essential Android tips	154
BlackBerry explained	156
Microsoft Windows 7 phone	158
Choosing the right one for you	160
Buying a smartphone	164
Setting up a smartphone	166
Smartphone security	170

ⓑ GETTING ONLINE

Going online with mobile broadband	74
Mobile broadband on your laptop	180
Mobile broadband on other devices	182
Going online using Wi-Fi	184
Using Wi-Fi when out and about	186
Using Wi-Fi on your mobile devices	188
Set up a home wireless network	189
Set up wireless and 3G on a Kindle	192
Synchronise your devices	193
Sharing media across devices	196

ⓑ PROTECTION

Mobile devices buying advice	202
Protect your mobile devices	205
Encrypt information on your laptop	206
Accessories for your mobile device	208

ⓑ RESOURCES

Jargon buster	214
Index	219

EDITORIAL NOTE

The instructions in this guide refer to the latest versions of the operating systems used by a specific device, including Microsoft Windows 7, Apple iOS and Google Android.

Screenshots are used for illustrative purposes only.

Microsoft Windows 7, Apple iOS and Google Android are American products. All spellings on the screenshots and on the buttons and boxes in the text are therefore spelled in US English. The rest of the text remains in UK English.

All technical words in the book are either discussed in jargon busters within the text and/or can be found in the Jargon Buster section on page 214.

INTRODUCTION

There has never been a better time to ditch the wires and embrace mobile computing. From laptops, netbooks and tablet PCs to smartphones and ebook readers, there's a wide choice of mobile computing devices on offer today.

Lightweight and portable, these devices typically combine powerful computer features with wireless internet access, so you can surf the web, read email, do general everyday computing, play games and listen to music, all while on the go. Some include the ability to make phone calls across the mobile phone network, while others allow you to read digital versions of your favourite books and magazines.

But, with so many different types available, choosing the perfect device for you can be daunting.

Laptops and Mobile Devices Made Easy is designed to guide you through everything you need to know when buying and using a laptop or mobile device.

With dedicated chapters on laptops, tablet PCs, smartphones and ebook readers, this book gives clear guidance on the must-have features of today's mobile devices. With examples from the most established devices on the market, there's also helpful advice and step-by-step instructions on using and getting the most from your laptop or mobile device.

Later chapters show you how to get online: from setting up a wireless network and mobile broadband, to using your device to connect to the internet while out and about. Other topics include synchronising and sharing files and media across all your equipment, advice on how to protect them and jargon busters to help demystify technical terms.

In combination with other books in the series, such as *Computing Made Easy for the Over 50s: Windows 7 Edition*, you'll be amazed at what you can achieve on your laptop or mobile device. And if you get stuck, you can contact the Which? Computing Helpdesk. Simply go to www.which.co.uk/computinghelpdesk and input code LAPTOPMOB311 where it asks for your membership number.

LAPTOPS & NETBOOKS

By reading and following all the steps in this chapter, you will get to grips with:

 Choosing the right laptop for you

 Essential features and connectivity

 Setting up your laptop

Laptops & Netbooks

LAPTOPS AND NETBOOKS EXPLAINED

Many people buy a laptop or a netbook as a replacement for an older, desktop PC, or as a handy second PC. Both are suitable if you need a small, portable computer that frees you from being tied to a desk.

What is a laptop?

A laptop is a small, lightweight computer that has a built-in screen, a keyboard and a rechargeable battery – and you can use it how and where you want, without the hassle of cables or even a desk to sit it on.

Laptops run the same software as desktop PCs, and many are powerful enough to do everything from email and surfing the web, to photo and video editing, to playing the latest games. Provided there is enough charge in the battery, you can work away from a mains socket either at home or when travelling. You can even connect to the internet on the go so that you can remain in touch with friends and family via email and social networking sites.

What is a netbook?

A netbook is a mini-laptop. Weighing around 1kg (2.2lbs) or less, and with screen sizes ranging from 6–10in (15–25cm), they are lighter than a laptop and easier to carry around.

Most netbooks contain a different type of processor from traditional laptops, one designed specifically for smaller mobile devices (see page 18). Netbooks typically come with less memory (Ram) and less storage than laptops, and have integrated (and less powerful) graphics chips (see page 28), which make them less suitable for gaming or image-intensive computing. As a netbook is smaller than a laptop, it is likely to have either a smaller-than-standard-size keyboard or one that has the keys sitting closer together.

A new type of netbook is emerging that aims to deliver both a netbook and tablet PC (see page 68) in a single device. Hybrid netbooks (shown above) offer full keyboard and standard netbook features, but have a special screen that can be flipped over, and the lid closed against the keyboard with the screen still accessible. The screen is touchscreen, allowing it to be used as both netbook and tablet.

Netbooks are cheaper than laptops, and designed primarily for email and surfing the web, as well as basic office tasks. Although they lack built-in optical drives for CDs or DVDs, netbooks do include built-in wireless connectivity, making them perfect for people on the go who want internet connectivity without lugging around a heavier, full-sized laptop.

Laptops & Netbooks

BENEFITS OF BUYING A LAPTOP

If you're in two minds about whether a laptop is right for you, here are some of the benefits that a laptop or netbook have over a traditional desktop PC.

In the home

If you are thinking of buying a new computer for the home, you may consider buying a laptop rather than a PC.

Save space More people now buy a laptop as their main home computer. Laptops offer similar features to a desktop PC, yet, because they are designed to be portable, they can be easily moved from room to room. Laptops are a great space saver – a real benefit over traditional desktop PCs. And if you've got kids, you can keep an eye on what they're up to when using a laptop by having it in the same room as you.

Save money Small, cheap laptops give you access to the internet and PC software, but without the price tag of buying a desktop computer and monitor. Netbooks start from around £150, while full-sized budget laptops can cost as little as £250.

Work and play from anywhere Choosing a laptop means you can take advantage of wireless networking to surf the internet without being tied to a phone socket – so you can send emails or play games while sitting on the sofa, or even in the garden.

Get creative Combining a laptop with your digital camera and video camcorder means it can be used for editing family photos and videos. Transferring music to an MP3 player can keep you tuned in to the latest sounds, while you store your albums on your laptop.

Have fun Some of today's laptops have powerful graphics that can play modern computer games. To surround yourself in sound, you can connect external speakers to laptops, or add a set of headphones for more personal game playing.

On the go

Stay in touch Most laptops include a webcam, making it simple to stay in touch with friends and family by using video conferencing. Video software can allow free video calls between laptops or PCs anywhere in the world.

Travel light Laptops are small and light, and netbooks lighter still. Weighing less than a large paperback, netbooks offer many of the features of a full-blown laptop. And, with screens of around 9in (23cm), carrying them is a breeze.

Keep entertained Many laptops include DVD and even Blu-ray disc drives, so you can watch the latest movies while travelling – ideal for long train journeys, or keeping the kids entertained on a car trip.

Stay connected Public Wi-Fi hotspots (see page 184) allow you to connect your laptop to the internet for free. Some shops and cafes offer customers Wi-Fi access. And, even if you are not near a hotspot, laptops can connect to the 3G mobile network (see page 174) to access the internet, although this can cost around £10 a month to use.

Laptops & Netbooks

LAPTOPS TOUR

SCREEN
Laptops benefit from a range of screen sizes – from 12in (30.5cm) up to 17in (43cm) and even larger. Laptops can have high-resolution screens capable of displaying high-definition (HD) films played back from Blu-ray drives, or directly from the hard drive. Most laptop screens have a glossy finish, which makes colours appear brighter and more vibrant – good for playing games or watching movies. Some laptops screens have a matt finish, which helps to reduce glare caused by bright lights.

KEYBOARD
Most laptops include a full-sized keyboard similar to one you might use with a desktop PC. However, most lack a dedicated number keypad, and some keys serve dual functions, such as also dimming the screen brightness.

TRACKPAD
Laptops have large trackpads that control the cursor on the laptop screen. Some trackpads allow multi-touch control, such as sliding two fingers across the surface to scroll through a document. Trackpads typically include two buttons that mimic the left and right buttons on a desktop PC mouse.

WEBCAM
Webcams are fairly standard on laptops, and are used for video calls and taking low-resolution photos.

AUDIO AND MEDIA
Laptops often have reasonable speakers, but they will not rival those on a desktop PC. Many also include media buttons above the keyboard which control volume and media playback, as well as allowing instant access to the internet.

PORTS AND CONNECTIONS
Laptops have lots of connectivity options, especially compared to a netbook. See page 16 for a guide to laptop connections.

OPTICAL DRIVE (NOT SHOWN)
Expect modern laptops to include a DVD optical drive that can burn DVDs as standard. This is handy for storing home movies and photos. Some expensive laptops include a Blu-ray disc drive that can be used to play Blu-ray movies on the laptop's screen.

NETBOOKS TOUR

SCREEN
Due to their small size, netbook screens tend to range from 9–11in (23–28cm), and their lower cost means the screens are not the best quality. Screen resolution is low, too, meaning that you can't fit as much on the screen as you can with a laptop.

KEYBOARD
Due to their small frame, keyboards are one of the shortcomings of netbooks. Instead of a full-sized keyboard, most netbooks include a reduced-size version, usually around 90 per cent the size of a traditional keyboard. Many keys will be far smaller than normal, and there is little space for dedicated buttons for media playback or for controlling the screen, such as brightness controls.

TRACKPAD
Netbooks feature tiny trackpads which, while saving space, do mean that controlling the cursor on the screen can be a bit fiddly. And, unlike laptops, many netbooks feature a single button on a rocker beneath the trackpad that mimics the left and right buttons of a desktop PC mouse, depending on the side that is pressed.

WEBCAM
Webcams are fairly standard on netbooks, and are suitable for video calling and taking low-resolution photos.

AUDIO AND MEDIA
Don't expect top-notch audio with a netbook – Which? tests show that the tiny speakers in a netbook can sometimes produce a 'tinny', weak sound. Netbooks don't have powerful media features, either.

PORTS AND CONNECTIONS
Netbooks have a basic range of ports and connections, such as USB, which are satisfactory for day-to-day computing.

OPTICAL DRIVE
Netbooks do not include optical drives, such as DVD (see page 13).

PORTS

Laptops and netbooks can come with a bewildering array of ports and slots. Here is an explanation of some common ports.

FireWire

A common connection option. It's fast and suitable for transferring large amounts of data from devices, such as video footage from a camcorder.

S-video out

An acronym for Super-Video, a technology for transmitting video signals over a cable. This port allows you to connect your laptop to a television.

VGA

This allows you to connect your laptop to an external monitor or projector, so the image on the screen can either be repeated ('mirrored'), or you can extend the desktop area of your laptop using the extra monitor screen, giving you space to view more programs.

USB 2.0

This port is used to connect to a wide variety of peripherals, such as mice and digital cameras. Most laptops have more than one, but check there are enough to connect all your peripherals, plus a spare for using a memory stick.

Ethernet (RJ-45)

This allows you to plug in an ethernet cable, and so connect your laptop to another computer, a local area network (LAN), or a modem for connecting to the internet.

Modem

This port offers an alternative to wireless connection for occasional internet access. Most modern laptops don't include a modem port, relying instead of either ethernet or Wi-Fi connectivity.

Parallel

Used to connect to a printer, though many modern laptops use USB.

Audio in
Plugging a microphone into this allows you to import sound to your laptop.

Audio out
Compatible headphones and external speakers can be plugged in here.

Memory card slot
There may be one or more slots for different types of memory cards – a form of removable storage used by devices such as digital cameras and camcorders. Removing the card from the device and inserting it into the slot allows you to quickly transfer files without the need for connection cables. Slots may include SmartMedia, CompactFlash, SD and ExpressCard slots.

Jargon buster

Memory stick
These are small, portable devices used to transfer and store data. They plug into USB ports and are also referred to as flash pen drives, USB keys or pen drives.

Laptops & Netbooks

PROCESSORS

Buying a laptop will bring you face-to-face with a few technical specifications, which can seem confusing. Here's a list of some of the key parts of a laptop – and what you need to know about them when choosing a model.

Laptop processors

Also called the CPU (Central Processing Unit), the processor is the brain of your laptop, performing all of the calculations that make the computer work. The more powerful the processor is, the faster your laptop or netbook will run. The speed of a processor – that is the number of instructions per second that it can carry out – is measured in gigahertz (GHz).

There are two main manufacturers of computer processors – Intel and AMD. Regardless of a laptop brand, size or price, usually one of these processors will be found inside. Apple MacBooks and most Windows laptops use the Intel Core Duo and Intel Core family of processors.

Both processors perform everyday tasks perfectly well. The equivalent AMD chip is usually slightly cheaper, which does help lower the overall cost of the laptop. However, most laptops on sale use Intel chips, as these are the most popular type of chips for powering PCs.

Processor types

Some of the processors commonly used in laptops and netbooks include:

- **Intel Atom** is a processor specially designed for small mobile devices, such as netbooks, and which enables essential basic computing tasks
- **AMD NEO** is AMD's counterpart to the Intel Atom, again designed specifically for netbooks to enable essential, basic computing tasks
- **Intel Celeron M** is a good processor for standard computing tasks and performance. Typically found in ultra-portable, basic and family laptops
- **AMD Sempron Mobile** is good for basic tasks and performance. It is typically found in ultra-portable, basic and family laptops
- **AMD Athlon 64 Mobile** a general performance chip suitable for everyday use
- **Intel Core Duo / Core 2 Duo** are powerful processors typically found in mid-range and general everyday laptops
- **AMD Turion 64** is a powerful processor for high-end performance
- **Intel Core** is Intel's latest range of processors designed to replace its Core 2 Duo range of chips in mid-range and more powerful laptops

Multi-core processors

Also consider the number of cores a processor has. A multi-core processor effectively has more than one CPU on a single silicon chip, so it's better able to handle multiple tasks at once. A typical example is an Intel Core processor.

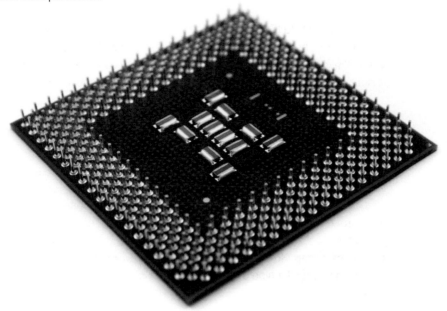

Nearly all laptops now come with dual-core processors. This means they have two processors inside that work together, so that your laptop works faster and can do more tasks at once.

Some high-end laptops come equipped with quad-core CPUs, but these expensive models are typically aimed at professional users, or those looking for a powerful gaming computer.

Processor speed

The speed of the processor plays a big part in the performance of your laptop. If you're looking for high-performance, go for a faster processor, and 2.5GHz or above is recommended for a good, all-purpose laptop.

Netbooks are the exception. These typically use Intel's Atom processor, which helps to boost the computing power while preserving battery life, but it's not as fast as a dual-core processor.

MEMORY AND DRIVES

Memory (Ram)

Ram (random access memory) is your laptop's short-term memory. It's used to store information while you're using the laptop (the laptop's hard drive is used for long-term file storage only). Consequently, the amount of Ram your laptop has determines how many different tasks it can accomplish simultaneously.

Aim to have as much Ram as you can afford – ideally at least 1GB, or 2GB if you will be running Microsoft Windows 7. This will make it easier to perform lots of computing tasks at the same time, such as playing music while you're surfing the internet, updating your security software, and sending and receiving emails.

It's usually possible to add more Ram to your laptop (see page 60).

Hard drive

Your laptop's hard drive (also known as a hard disk) provides long-term memory for your files and software, and its size is measured in gigabytes (GB).

A minimum of 100GB hard disk space is essential, so you can store plenty of photos, videos, music, and files. If in doubt, go for more hard drive space if you can afford it – many laptops include at least 250GB as standard. If, in time, you begin to run out of hard disk space on your laptop, you can upgrade to a newer, larger internal hard disk (see page 63). Alternatively, consider storing some of your files, such as photographs or movies, on an external hard disk drive.

Solid state drives

Some laptops – particularly netbooks – use solid-state storage, rather than a conventional hard disk, to store data. This uses less power and, unlike a traditional hard disk, has no moving parts, so it is faster and more durable.

At the moment, solid state drives (SSDs) cannot offer the same capacities as hard drives, so you may have to compromise on storage space. If you're only carrying out general office tasks, this shouldn't be a problem, but large files, such as video clips, could soon use up the space. The capacity of SSDs is generally up to about 64GB – fine for many users' needs – but tiny compared with typical laptop hard drives which offer around 500GB.

Laptop optical drives
Most laptops come with a CD and DVD drive of some kind for playing music CDs and video and software DVDs.

Many laptops come with a multi-format burner, so you can create your own CDs and DVDs, too. These drives can record to a variety of blank DVDs (DVD-R, DVD-RW and DVD-RAM), as well as CDs (CD-R and CD-RW).

A DVD drive is preferable to a CD drive, as a DVD can hold much more data. DVD drives are useful for making your own video DVDs, as well as for backing up large amounts of data.

Newer laptops include a Blu-ray drive so you can watch high-definition (HD) films on the move.

AT-A-GLANCE GUIDE TO OPTICAL DRIVES

Your laptop may have one or more of the following:
- ▶ **CD-ROM drive** reads CDs such as music CDs and computer software CDs.
- ▶ **CD-RW drive** records onto a blank CD, as well as reading it.
- ▶ **DVD ROM drive** stores up to 4.7GB of data. Plays films as well as reading CDs.
- ▶ **DVD-RW drive** records onto a blank DVD, as well as reading it.
- ▶ **BD-ROM drive** reads Blu-ray discs with high-definition (HD) video or data. Usually able to play and write to CD and DVD media too.
- ▶ **BD-RW drive** records onto a blank Blu-ray disc, as well as reading it. Usually plays and writes to CD and DVD media too.

TIP
Slot-load drives are preferable to tray-mounted drives, as they're less prone to breakage.

laptops & netbooks

Laptops & Netbooks

SCREEN

All laptops come with their own built-in LCD screens. There are several elements to take into consideration when selecting a laptop screen, including the size, pixel resolution, and glossy versus matt appearance of the screen.

Screen size

When shopping for a laptop, start by thinking about your ideal screen size. Screen size is measured by diagonal length, and most laptop screens will range from 8 to 20in (20.25 to 51cm). For everyday use, the most common size is around 15in (38cm). Opt for a larger 17in- (43cm-) screen if movies and games matter to you, or choose a 10in- (25.5cm-) screen if you want a portable netbook.

The dimensions of the screen will usually dictate the overall size and weight of the laptop. A larger screen will mean a bigger, heavier laptop, so it pays to think ahead about how you will use it. Carrying around a large 17in (43cm) laptop will prove cumbersome, while paying extra for an ultra-portable model with a small screen that never leaves your desk is a waste of money.

A good compromise is a 15.4in (39cm) widescreen laptop. Many models are available with this screen size and, weighing in at around 3kg (6.6lb), offer a good balance between usability and portability.

Screen dimensions

When looking at laptop screens, you will probably encounter information about the screen's aspect ratio.

Aspect ratio refers to the number of horizontal pixels to vertical pixels in a display. Traditional screens used a 4:3 aspect ratio, but most new laptops feature a widescreen display that uses either a 16:10 or 16:9 aspect ratio. Known as True Widescreen, 16:9 is the ratio typically used for high-definition (HD) televisions.

Watching movies, playing games, and even day-to-day computing tasks that involve several program windows open at once, are all much easier and more enjoyable on a widescreen display. When watching video on your laptop, you'll avoid that annoying black strip above and below the image being shown.

Some expensive laptops have ultra-wide screens. These have a near 2:1 width to height measurement, but this can make for awkward viewing of general content.

Screen resolution
This refers to the number of pixels on the screen itself – and is usually listed with horizontal pixels first, and vertical pixels second.

For example, a standard screen size is 1,680 x 1,050 pixels. The more pixels (and the higher the numbers) you have, the sharper the overall image of your screen and the more information you can show on the screen at once.

High-definition movies and 3D games look great on a high-resolution screen.

Glossy versus matt
Laptops typically come with a glossy screen, which delivers bright and vivid colours – great if you're watching films or viewing family photographs.

If you plan to regularly use your laptop outdoors, or somewhere where there's lots of glare, then look for a laptop with a matt screen to avoid irritating screen reflections.

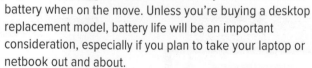

BATTERY

While all laptops can be plugged into the mains, they use an internal battery when on the move. Unless you're buying a desktop replacement model, battery life will be an important consideration, especially if you plan to take your laptop or netbook out and about.

Most laptops today use Lithium-ion (Li-ion) batteries that typically last three hours, although newer models can extend this to around five hours. Netbook batteries last longer – up to eight hours.

Be aware, however, that you're unlikely to match the manufacturer's claimed battery life when using your laptop. Watching a DVD or using the wireless (Wi-Fi) connection will drain the battery more quickly than day-to-day office tasks.

If you're concerned about the extending your battery life, for example when using it away from home or the office, use the settings designed to optimise your laptop's power options. Here's how:

Optimise a laptop's power settings in Windows 7

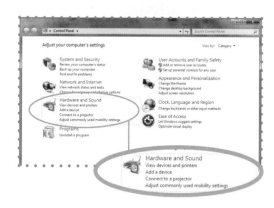

1 Click **Start**, and then **Control Panel**

2 In the Windows Control Panel, click on **Hardware and Sound** and then **Power Options**

3 Click the Power saver button. Then click **Change plan settings**

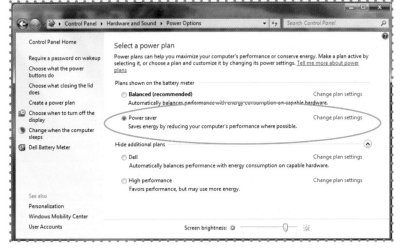

4 In this window you can change the sleep and display settings both when using the battery and when connected to the mains. To maximise battery life, reduce the time before the screen is dimmed and turned off, along with the put-into-sleep mode

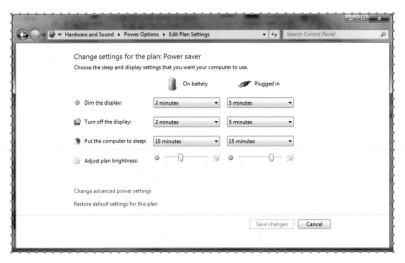

5 Use the slider to adjust the screen brightness: making it dimmer, but still readable, will help to conserve battery life

Laptops & Netbooks

Tips to help extend battery life

If you take care of your laptop battery, and take steps to prolong its life, you can be confident that it will be ready to work properly when you need it most.

▶ **Avoid extreme temperatures** Don't leave a laptop outside in cold weather, or in a hot car. Cold batteries can't create much power and hot batteries will discharge quickly

▶ **Concentrate on one task at a time** Don't have lots of programs open and running at the same time, as this will quickly drain battery life

TRY THIS

If the battery in your laptop degrades over time, consider swapping it for a newer battery. See page 66.

▶ **Watch your computer activities** If you need to preserve the life of your battery while using your laptop on the move, be careful what you use it for. Activities such as email and word processing use much less power than playing a game or watching a movie on DVD, or streamed across the internet (see page 188 for an explanation of streaming)

▶ **Ditch external devices and connections** USB devices such as a mouse and Wi-Fi will drain your laptop battery. So, if necessary, remove or shut them down when not in use

▶ **Charging your laptop** Fully charge the battery whenever you have access to a power source

▶ **Keep it clean** Clean your battery's metal contacts every couple of months using a cotton swab, the tip of which has been dipped in rubbing alcohol. This makes the transfer of power from your battery more efficient

▶ **Remove the battery** If you're using a laptop as a desktop replacement, and it's constantly plugged into the mains, consider removing the battery. Constantly charging the battery will reduce its lifecycle. Remove the battery – making sure that it is charged to 40 per cent – and store it in a dry, warm place

▶ **Buy another battery** Some laptops can run with two batteries, although this adds to the size and weight of your computer. If you can't do this, check with your laptop's manufacturer to see if high-capacity batteries are available for it. Alternatively, buy an external battery from a computer store, which will help to extend the operating time

INPUT DEVICES
Keyboards
Predictably, laptop keyboards are smaller than those that come with a desktop computer. The keys themselves are closer together, and they may be smaller. Because the keyboard is built into the body of the laptop, you may find that it's not as comfortable to use as a desktop keyboard, which can be repositioned to suit you.

Netbook keyboards are smaller still, and you're likely to find that the keys are even closer together. Some keys may also have been moved in order to fit everything in, while others – usually the cursor keys and the right shift key – may have been reduced in size.

It's a good idea to try out a laptop's keyboard before you buy, to ensure you get one you're comfortable with.

Trackpads and touchscreens
Laptops don't include a computer mouse. Instead, they have other input devices for navigating a cursor around the screen, such as trackpads (also known as touchpads, shown right) and even touchscreens.

A trackpad is a square-shaped, touch-sensitive area located below the space bar of a laptop keyboard. Moving a finger across the trackpad moves the cursor across the screen. Typically, one or two clickable buttons at the front of the touchpad act like mouse buttons.

Some more recent laptops also allow you to touch the screen directly to control on-screen elements, such as opening files, launching programs, and accessing menus. Known as touchscreens, these work in the same way as tablets (see page 68) for controlling the screen – although reaching out and pointing, dragging and tapping the screen of a laptop can be tiring. Touchscreen laptops are relatively rare at present.

Bear in mind, though, that all laptops and netbooks also allow you to plug in a standard computer mouse, typically using the USB port.

GRAPHICS

All laptops come with a graphics chip or card – known as a GPU (graphics processing unit) or video card – that's designed to handle the graphics you see on screen. Two types of cards are available – either an integrated graphics card, such as ones from Intel, or a dedicated graphics card, from companies such as Nvidia and ATI.

The difference between the two types mainly comes down to memory. Integrated graphics cards work by borrowing a part of the laptop's main memory – its Ram – whereas a dedicated graphics card has its own supply of Ram. Using its own Ram means that a dedicated graphics card is more powerful and faster than an integrated graphics card. Dedicated graphics cards have also been specially tuned to handle screen graphics faster, and can power more visually complex games.

Choosing between the two types comes down to what you will use your laptop for, and budget. For general word processing, email and other day-to-day tasks – and for those on a budget – an integrated video card is a good option.

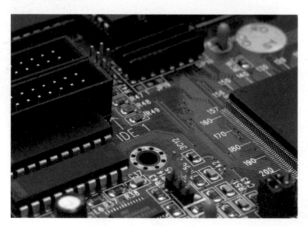

For playing more modern games, such as 3D racing games, and for users wishing to use their laptops for video and image editing, it's best to go for a laptop with a dedicated graphics card.

The best graphics cards have advanced 3D graphics chips along with 512MB to 1GB of dedicated graphics memory. For other less onerous tasks, a graphics card with 128MB to 256MB of its own memory should be sufficient.

Expect to pay more (from around £700) for a laptop with a dedicated graphics card.

Be aware, though, that these powerful graphics cards generate a lot of excess heat, which is why it's impossible to combine high-end graphics in the smaller frame of laptops such as netbooks. Entertainment laptops, with huge screens, are usually the heaviest, most expensive models.

SOUND

Most laptops include an integrated sound card and come with built-in speakers – although you may find some ultra-portable models that don't have speakers.

Don't expect to be blown away by the sound quality of laptop speakers – laptop speakers are generally adequate for playing MP3s, watching DVDs and most other tasks. While some high-end laptops do feature advanced, brandname speakers and subwoofers, generally sound isn't a selling point for any laptop.

If you can't bear to be without top-notch audio, make sure your laptop has a line output so you can easily connect external speakers. Laptops usually have 3.5mm (0.13in) audio jacks for plugging in headphones, and some have an integral microphone, which can be used for internet phone calls through Voice-over-Internet-Protocol (VoIP) providers such as Skype. These allow you to make telephone calls over the internet, rather than using the standard telephone network.

TRY THIS

The quickest way to change the volume on Windows laptop speakers is to click the Speakers button in the notification area of the taskbar, and then move the sliders up or down to increase or decrease the speaker volume.

laptops & netbooks

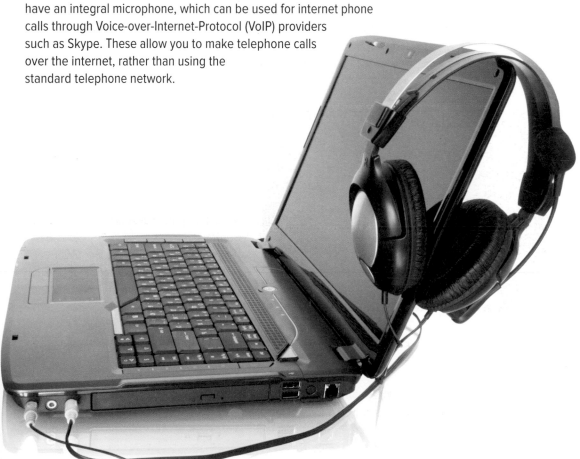

Laptops & Netbooks

WEBCAMS

A webcam is a tiny digital camera that's usually built into your laptop – generally they are positioned just above the screen, and facing you as you look at the screen.

Webcams are a fun tool that allow you to see other people who are connected to the internet in real-time. Webcams are mainly used for chatting to friends and family, or for business video-calls, but they also let you capture photos and video, and play them across the internet.

As with telephone calls, both you and the person you wish to talk to will need the same type of equipment – a webcam and an internet connection.

Even the best built-in webcams offer only two megapixels (Mp) resolution, although 1.3mp is typical on a netbook. If you prefer high-quality images, consider plugging in a separate USB webcam. There are lots of options available from Logitech, Creative Labs and Microsoft.

How to get the best from your webcam

▶ Make sure your webcam lens is dust free as this will help improve image clarity, but don't use your finger or a cloth to clean it. Instead, blast the lens with a burst of canned air to blow away debris

▶ Make sure your webcam settings – particularly brightness contrast, hue and saturation – suit the lighting in the room. To access your webcam settings, click **Start** and then **Control Panel**. Choose **Hardware** then double click your internal webcam from the hardware list. Select the **Properties** tab to open the setting controls and use the slider to adjust settings for your web broadcast

▶ Lighting is very important, so don't use your laptop screen as a light source. Turn on a main light or desk light, but don't direct it at your face – too much light close to the webcam can blanch the image, making it difficult to see. Always aim for diffuse light where possible

▶ Position yourself fairly close to, and directly in front of, the webcam lens, as they are not as good quality as those on camcorders. Also, keep the background simple and avoid distracting patterns or movements. If you plan to use your webcam a lot, consider buying a collapsible background disc from Amazon or a photographic supplier

▶ To help improve a webcam broadcast, try wearing a white shirt. This will help your webcam's auto white balance/auto-exposure achieve a good white balance and colour exposure

▶ If your webcam's image is too blurry, try lowering your screen resolution. To do this, right-click on your desktop and click **Properties**, and then **Screen Resolution**. Reduce the resolution to one level below its current setting and test the image quality. Repeat the process until you achieve the desired clarity

▶ Optimise the settings used in your video chat program. If you're using Skype, for example, select **Tools** and click on the **Video** icon in the left toolbar. Click **Webcam Settings** and adjust the visual and camera function settings as well as lighting compensation

▶ A minimum bandwidth connection of 1Mbps is required to broadcast a good-quality video session. So, check your bandwidth settings. If network traffic is high, or other users are sharing the same internet connection, it may lower the quality of your video projection. Visit an online test site such as www.speedtest.co.uk and run a bandwidth check

Jargon buster

Mbps
Mbps – or Megabits per second – are the units used to measure the speed at which data transfers across the internet. They are often used when talking about broadband speed.

Disabling your integrated webcam

There may be reasons why you wish to disable your integrated webcam. If you're a parent for example, preventing your children's access to video instant messaging and chat websites may be a priority. Here's how to disable your webcam in Windows 7:

1 Click **Start** on the taskbar at the bottom of your desktop and, from the right-hand list, click on **Control Panel**

2 Click on **Hardware and Sound**

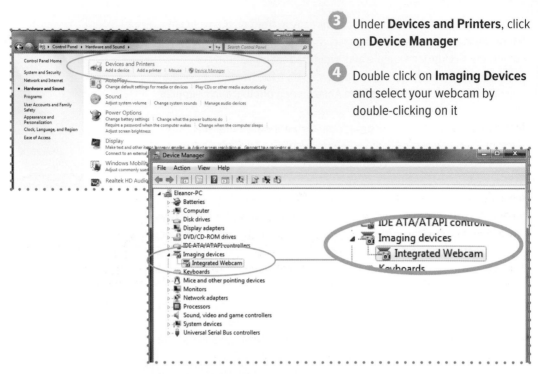

3 Under **Devices and Printers**, click on **Device Manager**

4 Double click on **Imaging Devices** and select your webcam by double-clicking on it

5 Click on the **Driver** tab and select **Disable** to disable the webcam

6 Click **Yes** when asked if you really want to disable it. Your webcam is now disabled. To re-enable the webcam, simply follow the above steps and then click on **Enable** in the window that appears in Step 5

NETWORKING FEATURES

Networking is a communication system that allows two or more computers to communicate with each other. The network can be created using a system of cables or Wi-Fi.

Wired ethernet networks

Most laptops include a socket for connecting to a wired (ethernet) network. This is also referred to as a 10/100/1000 LAN RJ45 socket.

Wireless network connectivity (Wi-Fi)

Most laptops include built-in wireless connectivity, known as Wi-Fi. This means that you can connect them to your existing home wireless network or go online at a wireless hotspot while out and about.

The best laptops will boast the latest and fastest wireless connections. See page 184 for more on Wi-Fi networks.

Laptop sockets

USB and FireWire Check that your chosen laptop has enough USB and FireWire ports to connect peripherals such as digital cameras, camcorders, printers, external keyboards, mice and hard drives. See page 16 for more information about ports.

Bluetooth If you want your laptop to communicate wirelessly with Bluetooth devices, such as mobile phones or wireless mice, then make sure that it has built-in Bluetooth. The alternative is to buy a separate USB Bluetooth 'dongle'. See page 180 for more information about dongles.

ExpressCard slots ExpressCard slots enable a variety of accessories to be plugged into a laptop. These include external hard and solid-state drives, wireless network (Wi-Fi) cards and TV tuner cards.

laptops & netbooks

Jargon buster

Computer interface
An interface refers to the programming code that allows software, such as applications, to talk to the computer hardware. It is also used to describe the appearance of screen menus and the controls you use to interact with the computer.

TRY THIS

To check whether your computer is running the 32-bit or 64-bit version of Windows on your computer, click **Start**, then **Computer**, then **Properties**. Under System type, it will say either '64-bit Operating System' or '32-bit Operating System' Operating System.

Jargon buster

32-bit and 64-bit processors
The terms 32-bit and 64-bit refer to the way a computer's processor (also called a CPU) handles information. A 64-bit CPU can work with larger amounts of random access memory (Ram) compared to a 32-bit CPU.

OPERATING SYSTEMS

One of the fundamental choices you need to make when buying a laptop is to decide which operating system you want to use. Operating system is the technical term for the software that controls a computer. This software manages the interface of your laptop or netbook, allowing you to use applications such as word processors, email programs and web browsers.

The two main computer operating systems are Microsoft Windows and Apple Mac OS X. Both look and work differently, and offer a range of benefits. They also run broadly the same range of software.

Microsoft Windows

Microsoft Windows is the world's most popular operating system, and is found on the majority of home and business laptops and netbooks, as well as desktop PCs. A wide range of software programs is available for Microsoft Windows and, as many other laptop owners also run Windows, finding help and answers to technical queries can be straightforward.

The majority of computer games are available for Microsoft Windows, which makes it suitable for families who are looking for a laptop for entertainment, as well as work and study.

The latest version of the Windows operating system is called Windows 7. It comes in three editions: Windows 7 Home Premium, Windows 7 Professional, and Windows 7 Ultimate. Most new laptops come with Windows 7 Home Premium pre-installed, although a few netbooks may come with the Starter edition instead.

All three versions of Windows 7 come in two formats; a 32-bit edition and a 64-bit edition. You'll find both in the box (on separate discs) if you buy the software yourself. The main difference is that the 64-bit edition has the potential to run faster and use larger amounts of system memory.

However, to install the 64-bit version of Windows, you need to make sure that your PC is 64-bit compatible. There's not always an obvious way to find this out; often the only way is to check with your PC's manufacturer. However, most modern laptops are powered by 64-bit processors, such as Intel's Core 2 Duo processor. Some older netbooks have 32-bit Atom processors, but the latest models now run 64-bit Atom processors.

If you enjoy using your laptop to watch, pause, and record live TV, play music, look at photos, and watch DVDs, then Windows 7's Media Center can help turn your laptop into a one-stop entertainment machine. This version has access to a broader range of TV channels, while the Turbo Scroll feature lets you zip through listings or a music library. A slideshow marker makes it easy to create slick photo presentations.

Laptop users benefit from Window 7's improved power management that helps squeeze more usage time from the battery. The processor and network adaptor (a computer hardware component that provides the interface between a computer and a network connection) go into standby when not in use, and the faster boot time means you spend less battery life waiting for your laptop to start up.

While Windows 7 is more secure than before, it still suffers from many viruses and spyware and so you will need to buy security software and keep it up to date (see page 56).

If you struggle with the smaller screen size of a laptop compared with a desktop monitor, several features in Windows 7 will help. These include:

▶ **Aero Shake** quickly cuts through the desktop. Grab the title bar of a window and shake it to minimize all other windows
▶ **Aero Snap** lets you quickly resize and rearrange windows so you can view two screens side-by-side

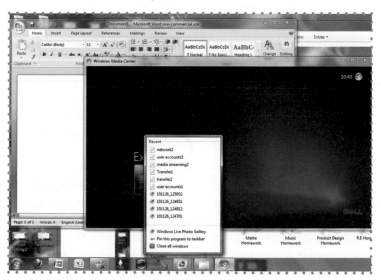

TRY THIS

While Microsoft Windows dominates the market, followed by Apple's Mac OS, Linux is a good alternative operating system, although the choice of laptops with this pre-installed may be limited.

Jargon buster

Boot time
Boot time is the length of time it takes for a laptop to start working from switching it on.

Virus
A virus is a destructive program that is transmitted from computer to computer within another program or file.

Spyware
Spyware is malicious software that, once on your laptop, may collect information about you, change settings or display pop-up ads when web browsing. Often installed through free software downloaded from the web, simply visiting a website can result in a spyware infection.

- ▶ **Aero Peek** is a timesaving feature that turns all of your open windows transparent so you can see the desktop beneath
- ▶ **Jump Lists** provide shortcuts to documents, pictures, songs, or websites that you use regularly
- ▶ **Taskbar** is now easier to see with larger icons, and you can 'pin' favourite applications on to any part of the taskbar to remain there whether open or not. You can click and drag icons to rearrange applications, and simply move your cursor over the icon to see previews of files
- ▶ **View Available Networks** makes it easy to view and connect to networks wherever you are. It displays all available wireless and wired options and then lets you connect with just a click

Apple Mac OS X

Apple Mac OS X (pronounced 'Mac OS Ten') is the operating system that runs Apple's MacBook range of laptops (see page 38), and is the second most popular system after Microsoft Windows.

Mac OS X is characterised by being easy to use, yet powerful. The simple interface shows elements such as folders, software and graphics in high fidelity. Many users say that this interface makes surfing the internet, checking email and using their laptop easier than with a Windows laptop.

Apple has included laptop-specific features in its operating system, including the ability to use multi-touch on the trackpad – this lets you pinch fingers together on the trackpad to zoom into a photo, for example. Mac OS X works seamlessly with the laptop – such as extending its battery life by turning off the hard drive when it isn't being used.

If you're concerned about viruses, Mac OS X is very secure and doesn't suffer from viruses and spyware to the extent that Windows laptops do. Mac OS X protects your laptop and data automatically, without needing to buy extra security software.

Mac OS X can run most of the programs available for Windows laptops, although you will need to buy special Mac OS X versions. Mac OS X also comes loaded with lots of applications to get you started, including managing your photos and music, surfing the internet and sending emails.

The next version of Apple's operating system is Mac OS X 10.7 (also known as 'Lion'), which is expected in the summer of 2011.

MacBook Air

This new version of the operating system will draw on features from Apple's mobile operating system iOS, which is used on the Apple iPhone and iPad, including greater use of multi-touch gestures, and its own App Store. See page 78 for more on the iPad.

WHICH OPERATING SYSTEM SHOULD I CHOOSE?

MAC OS X

Good for

- ▶ keeping your data and laptop free from viruses
- ▶ quick, easy navigation around your files
- ▶ getting started with lots of included software
- ▶ video, music and photography applications

Less good for

- ▶ having access to as much software as Windows
- ▶ getting a bargain; MacBooks are more expensive

WINDOWS

Good for

- ▶ lots of software to choose from
- ▶ works with many other laptops
- ▶ ease of use thanks to its familiar interface
- ▶ business applications and office software

Less good for

- ▶ stopping viruses getting access to your laptop
- ▶ working smoothly with your hardware (computer, screen and printer) at all times

APPLE MACBOOKS EXPLAINED

Apple MacBooks are a popular alternative to laptops from PC makers such as Dell, HP and Sony. MacBooks are available only from Apple – best known for its iPhone and iPod range of consumer products. Beneath the iconic design, MacBooks have similar specifications to other laptops, but have some features unique to Apple that make them a good – if expensive – alternative.

Apple MacBook range

Apple has a range of three MacBooks designed for different types of user, and at a range of price points. All MacBooks feature Intel processors and Nvidia graphics cards, along with a range of Ram and storage options. Screen sizes go from 11.6–17in (29.5–43cm), and prices start at £850.

Apple MacBook Apple's white-clad MacBook is aimed at the general consumer. It features a unibody design where the case is a single, continuous enclosure. It has a ten-hour battery life, and runs Mac OS X. It has a 13.3in (33.75cm) LED screen, weighs just over 2kg (4.4lb), and includes 2GB of Ram. Storage capacity varies depending on the specific model, and prices start from around £850.

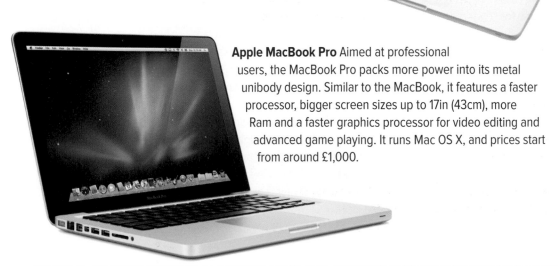

Apple MacBook Pro Aimed at professional users, the MacBook Pro packs more power into its metal unibody design. Similar to the MacBook, it features a faster processor, bigger screen sizes up to 17in (43cm), more Ram and a faster graphics processor for video editing and advanced game playing. It runs Mac OS X, and prices start from around £1,000.

Apple MacBook Air The latest entry into the MacBook range, the MacBook Air is Apple's answer to Windows netbooks in that it lacks an optical drive (both MacBook Pro and MacBook have DVD drives). Powered by an Intel processor, it is the thinnest laptop on the market. Weighing less than 1.5kg (3.3lb), its thinnest depth is a mere 3mm (0.07in). It is available in both 11- and 13-in (28- and 33-cm) screen sizes.

Apple MacBook features
Apple has lots of innovative features across its MacBook range, which help to set it apart from other laptop brands. These include:

Multi-touch MacBook trackpads let you use several fingers to pinch to zoom, two fingers to scroll, and twist and rotate objects.

Battery MacBooks are famed for their battery life – up to ten hours on some models. MacBook Air models can remain on standby for 30 days between charging, and feature an instant-on technology that means the laptop is ready for use immediately on opening the lid.

Illuminated keyboard Some MacBook models feature a light-up keyboard for typing in low-light conditions.

FaceTime All MacBooks feature a front-facing camera that uses a Wi-Fi connection to make free video calls to other FaceTime-compatible devices, such as other MacBooks, iPod Touches and iPhones.

▶ Laptops & Netbooks

DECIDING WHICH LAPTOP TO BUY

Laptops come in lots of sizes, and with different features – allowing you to choose the right one for your needs. While notebooks and small laptops are easy to carry and have a long battery life, they lack the features and speed of bulkier, desktop-replacement models. More powerful laptops are larger, and heavier, and take up more space.

To help you decide which laptop to buy, we'll first divide them into the following categories, from basic laptops to those to use for entertainment and games.

Basic laptop

Basic laptops offer lots of functionality, and are a good choice for families on a budget. Lacking some of the higher-end features, such as Media Center, and fast 3D graphics, most basic laptops will have a 15in (38cm) screen, DVD recorder, and be suitable for word processing, office software, web access, and photo editing.

Ideal as a second PC, look for one with a dual processor and at least 2GB of Ram, as well as Windows 7 Home Premium. A hard drive of at least 250GB is the norm with basic laptops. However, they tend to be heavy, and not too portable.

Average costs:
£250–£400
Brands: Acer, Dell, Lenovo, Packard Bell, Toshiba

Netbooks

Netbooks are tiny laptops. Some weigh less than 1kg (2.2lb), and are little more than 2.5cm (1in) thick. Their screens are usually 10in (25.5cm). They are suitable for surfing the web and working on general office or school documents. Their low cost, small size and portability makes them ideal for students and casual users.

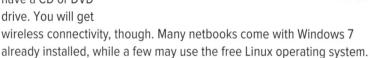

Their size means netbooks don't have full-size keyboards, and are less powerful than standard laptops. They use Intel Atom processors, and don't have a CD or DVD drive. You will get wireless connectivity, though. Many netbooks come with Windows 7 already installed, while a few may use the free Linux operating system.

Average costs: £200–£400
Brands: Acer, Asus, Dell, Toshiba, Samsung and Sony

Family laptop

Laptops with 17in (43cm) screens and larger are usually meant to be desktop PC replacements, and are great for the entire family. They can be heavy and awkward to move, but as their power and multimedia capabilities match those of traditional PCs, they make a good home computer.

With a large, usually wide-format, screen, a family laptop is ideal for those who want to edit photos or video and play games, as well as perform general office tasks.

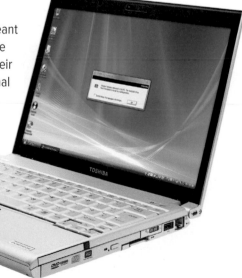

Average costs: £400–£700
Brands: Acer, Dell, Fujitsu Siemens, Samsung, Toshiba, Sony

laptops & netbooks

41

▶ Laptops & Netbooks

Business laptop

Ultra-portable business laptops make size and weight the priority, shrinking things down so they're easier to carry, but often at the cost of power, speed and features. What you gain in portability is offset by smaller keyboards and displays.

While ultra-portables use slower processors to conserve battery life, it shouldn't affect your productivity. Even a 1GHz processor is capable of running everyday office applications and basic photo-editing tasks with relative ease. They're more powerful than netbooks.

Average costs: £600–£1,000
Brands: Apple, HP, Sony, Toshiba

Entertainment laptop

If you want to use your laptop to play the latest video games, then you need a powerful system that's capable of handling high-end 3D games graphics. The ideal gaming laptop is fast with a large high-resolution screen. It will have at least 4GB of Ram and a large hard drive.

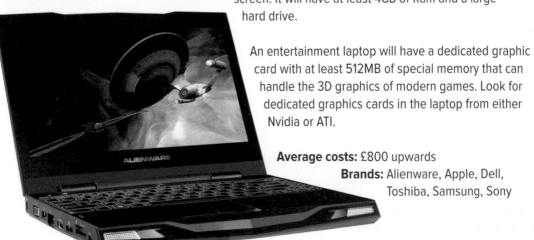

An entertainment laptop will have a dedicated graphic card with at least 512MB of special memory that can handle the 3D graphics of modern games. Look for dedicated graphics cards in the laptop from either Nvidia or ATI.

Average costs: £800 upwards
Brands: Alienware, Apple, Dell, Toshiba, Samsung, Sony

BUYING A LAPTOP: FACTORS TO BEAR IN MIND

When it comes to buying a laptop, one size doesn't fit all. The type of laptop you choose will depend on what you plan to use it for – and, with so many models to choose from, there's a laptop for every possible lifestyle. The guide below will help you choose the best type of laptop for your uses.

For families

Want a laptop that matches the power of your old, full-sized PC, but that can be folded away to save space, and even rid your room of a computer desk? Then look no further than a family or budget laptop.

These have the advantage of being portable (or at least luggable), and many of the more expensive models offer performance in line with decent desktop PCs. These are good models if your tasks include home finances, surfing the web, playing games, and photo and video editing.

A decent screen size and full-sized keyboard will ensure you can work or play in comfort, and plenty of ports ensure all your devices, such as cameras and camcorders, can be connected.

Go for
▶ A good-sized screen – 15in (38cm) display or larger
▶ Full-sized keyboard and trackpad
▶ 2GB of Ram and dual-core processor
▶ 250GB hard drive for storing digital photos and home movies

Don't worry about
▶ Weight and size
▶ Battery life

Recommended laptop type
▶ Family laptop
▶ Budget laptop

For professionals

If you plan to use your laptop when you're out and about to get that little bit of work done on the train, or stay connected on holiday without blowing your baggage allowance, then size and weight are the two most critical factors when choosing a laptop.

Laptops & Netbooks

Jargon buster

HDMI
High Definition Multi-media Interface (HDMI) is a digital connection capable of transferring uncompressed high-definition video and audio to your television or monitor. HDMI is the standard system used for connecting high-definition (HD) devices such as Blu-ray players, video games consoles and HD camcorders.

Look for a model that's small enough to fit in a bag or rucksack, and light enough that your back won't feel the strain. If you can afford it, choose an ultra-portable business laptop. Head for a wireless hotspot, or attach a mobile broadband dongle, and you can get online in most places.

Go for
▶ A lightweight laptop or netbook
▶ Good battery life, or the ability to swap batteries

Don't worry about
▶ A large screen
▶ Lots of storage
▶ Fast graphics and powerful audio

Recommended laptop type
▶ Netbook
▶ Ultra-portable business laptop

For entertainment

If you want to use a laptop for games then you'll need a laptop that supports high-end software. Choose a laptop with a dedicated graphics card from either ATI or Nvidia, and good connections such as HDMI if you want to connect it to a television.

To ensure games graphics look great, you'll need a screen of at least 17in (43cm) with a resolution of 1,600 x 1,200 pixels. Always buy a laptop that uses as fast a processor as you can afford. Faster processors drain battery life quicker, but you'll probably use this laptop near a mains supply.

Go for
▶ Dedicated ATI or Nvidia graphics card with 256MB or 512MB of its own memory
▶ 17in (43cm) screen
▶ Fast, dual-core processor
▶ 4GB of Ram

Don't worry about
▶ Battery life
▶ Portability

Recommended laptop type
▶ Family laptop
▶ Entertainment laptop

For students

Laptops are becoming increasingly popular with students. If your budget is tight, look for a laptop that delivers the most bang for your buck. All students need a model that's light and small enough to fit into a backpack, and be carried around comfortably.

Low-cost netbooks are a good choice as their main use will be for writing, email and connecting to the internet – but they are not suitable for playing games. Built-in webcams, software, security, and a decent amount of storage are important considerations.

Go for
▶ Lightweight if being carried around
▶ Fast processor if used at home
▶ Large hard drive for music collection

Don't worry about
▶ Screen size

Recommended laptop type
▶ Family laptop
▶ Netbook

GETTING THE BEST LAPTOP DEAL

Where to buy

It's important to do your research before buying a laptop. Start with a price comparison site or read Which? reviews, and get the best prices at www.which.co.uk.

On the high street It's worth going to a shop to try out the laptop you're interested in, even if you end up buying the same model online for less.

Make sure you like the feel of your chosen laptop, and that features such as the keyboard and the trackpad are comfortable to use. Ask yourself: How does the size of screen look? Does the machine feel light enough for my needs?

By phone Calling a mail order retailer means you can ask for advice, and you will often get a better price than from a shop. You can also ask for a discount, or free delivery, if you order there and then.

Online You'll find real savings online, but you'll have to navigate through computer jargon to get a cheap laptop deal. Clicking through a cashback website may save you even more money (up to 5 per cent).

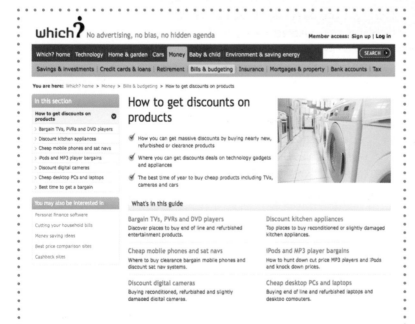

It is also worth considering slightly older or reconditioned models that are often sold at a discount online. See www.which.co.uk/discounts for a guide to online and outlet centres where you can buy last season's laptop, often at a large discount.

The downside of buying online is that you don't get to see your chosen model first hand.

'Free' laptops warning

Some shops will offer a 'free' or subsidised laptop when you sign up to a mobile broadband contract – usually 18 or 24 months – with some mobile phone companies (see page 181 for more on this type of deal). However, Which? has found that many of these deals will actually cost you more than buying the same laptop and mobile broadband separately.

Student savings

Laptop companies often advertise low-cost deals for students. Apple's student discount scheme, for example, can mean 6 per cent off an Apple MacBook Air, although discounts vary depending on the laptop you choose.

Check that these laptops really are the bargain they claim, as sometimes they're merely low-spec models, and by stretching the student loan a little further you can get a much better laptop.

Customised laptops

If you're on a tight budget, but want to spend a bit more making sure that you get the best performing laptop you can, aim to spend as much as you can afford on increasing the laptop's memory (Ram).

A decent processor is a good idea, but you don't need to go overboard getting the best chip on the market. Some manufacturers may offer special deals on older processors when, for example, they offer double the Ram for the same price.

Personal touch

Laptops are no longer limited to just grey, black, silver or white. You can now buy them in a range of fun colours such as such as pink, blue, green, orange, and purple – companies such as Dell offer this on some of their laptops. Some models are even customisable with different patterned covers.

Laptops & Netbooks

Jargon buster ▶

Driver
A piece of software that allows computers to communicate with devices such as printers.

SETTING UP YOUR LAPTOP

Once you've bought your new laptop, you'll need to set it up. Follow these tips to get started.

▶ Read and save all the instructions that come with your new laptop. This will include care, maintenance and which programs are included

▶ Give the laptop battery a full charge – this may take several hours. Don't be tempted to start your new laptop until this is completed, as it maximises the battery performance

▶ Turn on your laptop and follow the startup instructions. Typically, you'll be asked to create a user name, password and other user settings. See page 49 for more information on setting up a Windows account

TRY THIS

Make a System Repair Disc, which can help repair your Windows 7 laptop if a major error occurs. Open the Control Panel, click **System and Security**, then **Backup and Restore**. Click **Create a system repair disc**, then follow the on-screen instructions. Store this disc in a safe place.

▶ Make a note of the licence key for your laptop's operating system. This can be found on the card that came with the laptop, or the operating system CD if one is included. Store this information safely along with your laptop manual. Should your laptop crash, you will need this information to reinstall the operating system

▶ Install any programs or additional drivers that were shipped with your laptop. It's best to install one at a time, and re-start after each installation

▶ If you're using a Windows laptop, install a firewall and anti-virus program. See pages 56 and 57 for how to do this. Update all settings and run a scan on your laptop

▶ Set up your wireless internet connection. See page 50

▶ Once you're connected to the internet, check for software updates by visiting the manufacturer's website. Also check to see if there's an update to the OS as this will often fix minor bugs and problems

NEXT STEP ▶

For more on Windows 7, see *Which? Computing Made Easy for the Over 50s: Windows 7 Edition*.

▶ If you have software programs from an older desktop PC, use the discs to install them on your new laptop. Copy your existing computer files to your new laptop. See page 52 for how to do this in Windows 7

Create user accounts in Windows 7

When you first set up your Windows 7 laptop, you'll be required to create an administrator account and password. This is an access-all-areas pass that lets you set up your laptop and install programs. As anyone logged in as an administrator can make advanced changes, it's best to also create, and subsequently use, a standard user account to keep your laptop secure.

It's also best to give each family member their own separate, standard account. This will let you preserve your own settings and preferences, and set parental safety controls for younger family members.

Create a standard user account

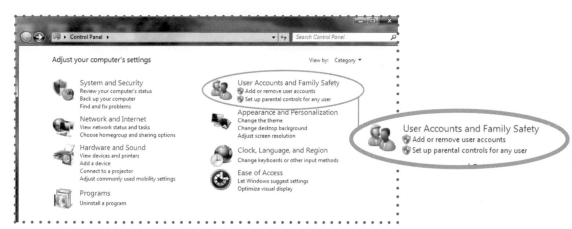

1 Click the **Start** button, the click the **Control Panel**, and then click **User Accounts and Family Safety**

2 Click **User Accounts**

3 Click **Manage another account**. If you're prompted for an administrator password or confirmation, type the password or provide confirmation

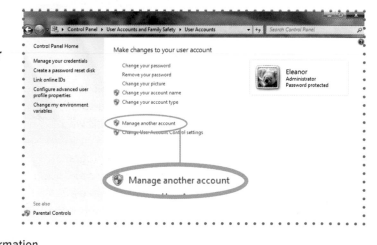

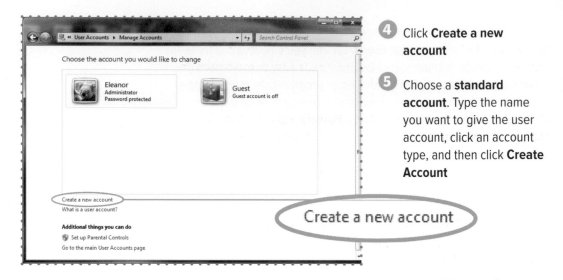

4 Click **Create a new account**

5 Choose a **standard account**. Type the name you want to give the user account, click an account type, and then click **Create Account**

Connect to the internet

One of the first things you will want to do with your new laptop is connect to the internet. If you have a laptop with built-in wireless connectivity, you'll be able to see a list of available wireless networks – including your existing wireless home connection – and then connect to one, no matter where you are. To learn how to set up a home wired and wireless connection see page 189.

To view and connect to available wireless networks

1 Open **Connect to a Network** by clicking the network icon at the right-hand side of the Taskbar

2 A list of available wireless networks will be shown in a pop-up window. Click on a network, and then click **Connect**

3 Many networks require a password to join. If this is the case, type in the password and click **Connect**

Set up a HomeGroup to share files and printers

The beauty of a home wireless network is that you can access the internet from any room in the house, and it also makes it easy to access files on other computers and printers wirelessly.

The easiest way to do this is to set up a HomeGroup – a group of computers that share pictures, music, videos, documents, and printers. To be in a HomeGroup, all the computers must be running Windows 7.

Create a HomeGroup

1 Click **Start**, **Control Panel**, and **Network and Internet**

2 Click **HomeGroup**

3 Click **Create a HomeGroup**. Choose which type of files you want to share (pictures, documents, music, videos and printers) and click **Next**

4 HomeGroup provides a password to help protect the shared files and printers. You can change that password at any time by following the steps in **Change a HomeGroup password**. You can also choose specific files and folders to share, or not share, with those who can access your HomeGroup. In your user account, select a file and click **Share with** from the toolbar at the top of the screen. Then choose from the options available and click **Share** when finished.

5 Once the HomeGroup has been set up, you can join it from any other Windows 7 PC or laptop on the network by clicking the HomeGroup entry in the left-hand pane of Explorer windows. The Join HomeGroup dialog box will automatically open. You will need to enter the password

TRY THIS

If you forget your HomeGroup password, you can find it by opening the HomeGroup window via the Control Panel. Then click **View or print the HomeGroup password**.

TRY THIS

If you change the HomeGroup password, update the new password on all the other HomeGroup computers as soon as possible so that they stay in sync.

Laptops & Netbooks

Jargon buster

Wizard
A wizard is a software tool that guides you through the steps of a process or task by asking a series of questions or presenting options.

MOVING DATA FROM YOUR OLD PC

If you've bought a laptop as a replacement for an older desktop PC, you will want to transfer your important files, email, pictures, and settings to your new laptop.

Windows 7 includes a program called **Windows Easy Transfer** that makes this task simple. Effectively a step-by-step wizard for transferring files and settings, Windows Easy Transfer lets you choose what to move to your new laptop, such as user accounts, internet favourites, and email. It also lets you decide which method to use, and then performs the transfer.

| **WATCH OUT!**
Windows Easy Transfer can transfer program settings, but not the programs themselves. These will need to be installed again from the original discs.

Welcome to Windows Easy Transfer

Windows Easy Transfer lets you copy files and settings from one computer to another. No information is deleted from your old computer.

You can transfer:

- User accounts
- Documents
- Music
- Pictures

- E-mail
- Internet favorites
- Videos
- And more

When the transfer is done, you'll see a list of what was transferred, programs you might want to install on your new computer, and links to other programs that you might want to download.

Tip: If you're upgrading this computer to Windows 7, think of "old computer" as referring to your "old version of Windows" and "new computer" as referring to your "new version of Windows."

Next

| **TRY THIS**
Transferring files can be a lengthy process so, if you've lots of files to move, it may be better to manually move large groups of data, such as movie or music folders, first. Then use Windows Easy Transfer to move the more personal data, such as email and bookmarks.

You can use Windows Easy Transfer to transfer files and settings from one PC running Windows XP, Windows Vista, or Windows 7 to another computer or laptop running Windows 7.

Transfer methods

There are a couple of ways to use Windows Easy Transfer to move files from one computer to another. The one you use depends on the equipment you have. Be sure to choose a method that works from both your old PC and your new laptop.

Easy Transfer Cable This USB cable works with Windows Easy Transfer to move information between computers. It cannot be used for any other purpose. The cable plugs into a USB port on each computer. They are sold by computer manufacturers and electronics stores.

Network To transfer files this way, the laptop and PC must be connected to the same network, and be able to access the same folders.

USB flash drive or external hard disk To use this method, you will need a USB flash drive or an external hard disk compatible with both computers. If you choose a USB flash drive, make sure it has enough storage.

Deciding on which method to use will depend in part on how many files you wish to transfer, and the speed of your computers. If you have a fast network, the networking option is a good choice. A wired network will provide faster data transfer than a wireless network, but the latest Wi-Fi standard 802.11n claims a fast data rate of up to 248Mbps. You will need a 802.11n router and computers capable of these speeds (see page 184). Check your manual or with the manufacturer. The Easy Transfer Cable option is equally good if you've a USB 2.0 port on both computers, although you will have to buy the cable. USB flash drives work well for a smaller number of files. In the example given here, we've used the external hard disk option.

Jargon buster

USB flash drive
A small portable device used to store and transfer data. It plugs into a USB port and is also called a USB key, flash drive or pen drive.

Getting started

1 Log on to both computers as an administrator

2 Install Windows Easy Transfer on your old computer. You can download this from Microsoft's website

3 Start Windows Easy Transfer on both computers. Click the **Start** button. In the search box, type Easy Transfer, and then, in the list of results, click **Windows Easy Transfer**

4 If you're prompted for an administrator password, type the password

Jargon buster

External hard drive
An external hard drive is a storage device that plugs into your computer. It is ideal for additional storage or saving (sometimes called backing-up) copies of important files.

On your old PC

1 Attach the external hard disk to your old PC

2 On your old PC in Windows Easy Transfer select a method of transfer
– in this case **An external hard disk**

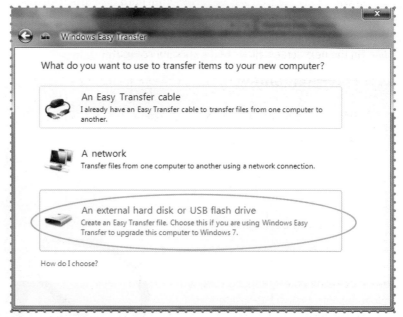

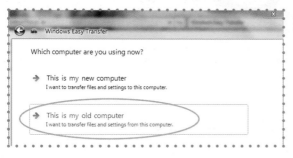

3 On the next screen click **This is my old computer**

4 Windows Easy Transfer scans the computer and automatically selects all the user accounts, files types and program settings

5 You can make changes to this selection if you wish, such as removing users' accounts by deselecting the tick box next to their name. Also, click **Customize** and, in the pop-up window that appears, clear any of the tick boxes next to files you do not wish to transfer

6 If you wish you can add a password to the transfer file

7 Then choose where on the external hard disk you want to save the file and click **Save**. The file will begin transfer

8 Once finished, disconnect the external hard drive

On your new laptop

1 In Windows Easy Transfer, select **external hard disk** as the method of transfer from the options available

2 On the next screen click **This is my new computer**

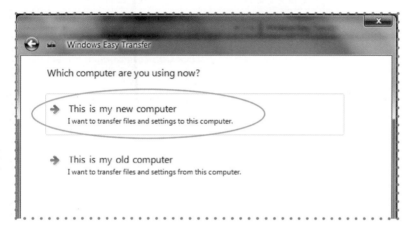

3 On the next screen select **Yes**, and plug in the external hard drive to your new laptop

4 Select the saved transfer file from the external hard drive and click **Open** to start the transfer

5 Once the transfer is complete, the program will show a report of what has been transferred and a list of programs that you may wish to install on your new laptop

Laptops & Netbooks

SECURE YOUR LAPTOP

Connecting to the internet, or sharing files with others, can leave your laptop open to security threats that could potentially damage your computer, or jeopardise your personal information. However, you can protect your laptop by installing the following software and keeping it up to date:

A firewall

This sits between your laptop and the internet, protecting your laptop from incoming attacks from hackers, or malware such as viruses. Windows Firewall is built into Windows, and should be turned on by default. To check that it is:

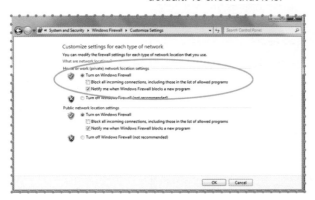

1 Click the **Start** button, and then click **Control Panel**. In the search box, type firewall, and then click **Windows Firewall**

2 In the left pane, click **Turn Windows Firewall on or off**. Type in the administrator password if required

3 Below each network location type, click **Turn on Windows Firewall**, and then click **OK**. It's best to turn on the firewall for all network location types

Anti-virus software

This helps to protect your computer against viruses, worms, and other security threats. Windows doesn't come with a built-in anti-virus program, but a free anti-virus program called Microsoft Security Essentials can be downloaded from the Microsoft Security Essentials website.

Many paid-for security suites are available. As new viruses are identified every day, it helps to use an anti-virus program with an automatic update capability. Updates usually require an annual subscription fee.

Alternatively, there are several free anti-virus programs available online. For example, AVG's free version of its anti-virus software can be downloaded from www.free.avg.com.

Jargon buster

Worm

A malicious program which spreads from computer to computer via the internet. Unlike a virus, it does not need to be attached to a document to infect a computer.

Anti-spyware software

This protects your laptop from spyware – malicious software that downloads to your laptop without your knowledge. Windows 7 has a built-in anti-spyware program called Windows Defender, which is turned on by default. It will automatically alert you when spyware tries to install itself on your computer. You can also use it to scan your laptop for existing spyware, which it will then remove.

Schedule a scan in Windows Defender

You can set Windows Defender to perform regular scans of your laptop. A daily quick scan will check the areas of your laptop that spyware is most likely to infect, while a full scan will check all files and programs.

1 Click the **Start** button. In the search box, type **Defender**, and then, in the list of results, click **Windows Defender**

2 Click **Tools**, then click **Options**

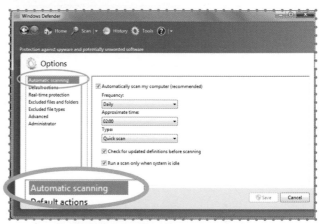

3 Under **Automatic scanning**, select the **Automatically scan my computer (recommended)** check box, select the frequency, time of day, and type of scan that you want to run, and then click **Save**. Type your administrator password if requested

4 To automatically remove spyware after a scan, in the left pane, click **Default actions**. Select the action that you want to apply to each alert item, select the **Apply recommended actions** check box, and then click **Save**. Type your administrator password if requested

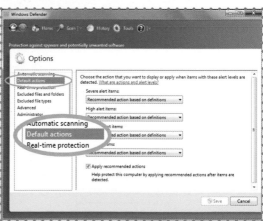

To protect your laptop against the latest spyware threats, Windows Defender needs to be regularly updated. To ensure the best level of protection, set Windows to install updates automatically (see page 58).

Operating system updates

It's a good idea to regularly check for updates to your operating system, as these can help protect your computer against viruses and other security threats. Rather than your hunting for information on Microsoft or Apple's websites, both Windows 7 and Mac OS X 10.5 can automatically check for software updates and let you know when one is available.

Turn on automatic updating in Windows 7

1 Click **Start**. In the search box, type **Update**, and then, in the list of results, click **Windows Update**

2 Click **Change settings**

3 Make sure **Install updates automatically (recommended)** is selected

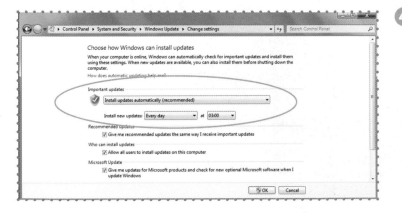

4 Under **Recommended updates**, make sure the **Give me recommended updates the same way I receive important updates** check box is selected, and then click **OK**. Type the administrator password if required

UPGRADING YOUR LAPTOP

The average lifespan of a laptop or netbook can be relatively short – anywhere from two to five years. A laptop that seemed fast and full of cutting-edge technology two or three years ago may now seem sluggish and outdated. But before rushing out to replace your existing laptop with a newer model, consider the possibility of upgrading some of its key components. Many high-street computer stores offer this type of upgrade, but with a little care and confidence you can upgrade simple components, such as memory, yourself.

Which components can be upgraded will vary by manufacturer and laptop model, but typically they include memory, hard disk, and battery.

Memory

Nearly all laptops allow for a memory (Ram) upgrade. This is usually done by opening a small compartment or door on the bottom of the laptop and adding, or removing and adding, a new memory strip. This is an affordable way to boost the power of your laptop, and Ram is usually the easiest component to upgrade.

Upgrading your laptop's Ram will dramatically improve its performance, and the more memory you upgrade to, the faster it can work. If you multitask, running two or three programs at the same time, you will quickly see an improvement after adding extra memory.

Ram comes in strips known as modules, which have different speeds and capacities. The hardest thing about upgrading your Ram is making sure you know what kind to buy, and how many free slots your laptop has (most computers have a limit as to how much Ram they can take).

TRY THIS

When upgrading any component that involves rooting around in your laptop, it's a good idea to first remove the laptop's battery. This will make sure all the electric current has dissipated from the system to avoid damage. See page 66 for how to do this.

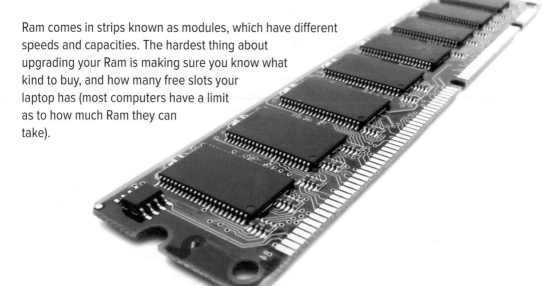

It's important to know that you can't just buy any memory and put it into your laptop. There are many different types of Ram, and the right type depends on the processor installed in your laptop.

Before you start, read the laptop manual to check the maximum memory capacity of your specific model. Then check how much is currently installed, and whether there's space for extra Ram.

TRY THIS

Unbranded memory is best avoided, the wrong memory or damaged memory chips can cause erratic system problems, and can even prevent your computer from booting. Try memory brands such as Danelec, Crucial and Kingston.

To check how much memory you already have installed, click on the **Start** button and then **Computer**. From the top menu click on **System properties**. You'll see details of your operating system and processor, as well as the amount of Ram installed.

How to buy Ram

There's plenty of choice as to where to buy extra memory as many companies make compatible Ram modules for different makes of laptop.

A good starting place is a computer memory specialist such as Crucial (www.crucial.com), which has an online tool to help you determine what memory is already installed, and what can be added, to your laptop.

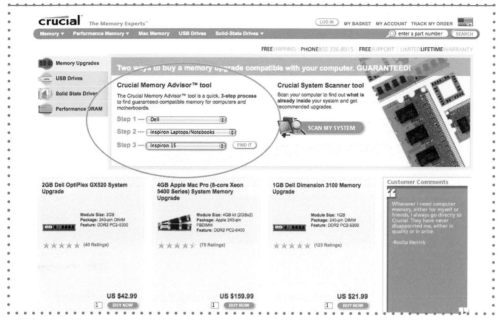

Simply enter the make and model of your laptop into Crucial's Memory Advisor Tool and it will automatically work out the best type of memory for your requirements.

Either buy memory directly from the online stores listed, based on the recommendations provided, or jot down the details and purchase your Ram elsewhere.

Add Ram to your laptop

1 Once your new memory has arrived, you're ready to install it. Before you go rooting around inside your laptop, however, you need to ensure that it's safe. Switch your laptop off at the mains and remove any cables

2 Remove the cover from the underside of your laptop using the correct sized screwdriver. You should now be able to see the free slot on the motherboard. If in doubt, see the laptop's manual

The memory slots are near the central processor – look for a cluster of thin slots about 5in (12.5cm) long. If you can't reach your existing Ram, then unplug from the motherboard any connectors that are in the way, making a note of how they go back in

Jargon buster

Motherboard
This is the large circuit board inside your laptop that various components plug into.

Laptops & Netbooks

3 Even the smallest of electrical charges can damage memory modules. To discharge any static, touch something metal before you start work and make sure you wear an anti-static wristband (these can be bought for as little as £5 from computer retailers)

4 Hold the Ram module on both sides, do not touch any of the contacts or the chips. Align the notches on the connecting edge of the next empty slot, and push down so the module sits squarely in the socket.

Make sure that the module is pushed firmly into the right slot. It's very easy to miss this, as it's still possible to close the side clips on the Ram module when even the main contacts are not connected.

The best thing to do is to push the memory in and down and, at the same time, move the clips to the side. Once it's fitted into place you should hear a 'click'

5 Ensure that the locking tabs have closed fully into place, then replace any connectors. Close the compartment flap and screw it into place

6 Turn your laptop back over and switch on. If the memory is slotted in correctly, you'll be able to start up and log on. Click the **Start** button, then **Computer**. Click on **System properties** to see the new amount of Ram that you've installed

UPGRADING YOUR LAPTOP HARD DRIVE

Most laptop hard drives (apart from some very slim ultra-portables) are 6.25cm (2.5in) wide and rotate at 4,200rpm, 5,400rpm, or 7,200rpm, with capacities of 250GB or more. All else being equal, the faster the spin rate, the better your laptop will perform.

When shopping for a replacement hard drive, the most important thing is to ensure it is compatible with your laptop. So, first check what type of hard drive is in your laptop.

Check the type of hard drive in your laptop

1 Click the **Start** button, then **Computer** and **System properties**

TRY THIS

Windows 7's Easy Transfer is a good alternative to using a USB-to-SATA cable and cloning software. It allows you to copy all your laptop files and settings onto an external hard disk before copying them onto the new hard disk drive once it has been installed. See page 52 for instructions for using the Windows Easy Transfer tool.

2 From the left-hand menu click **Device Manager**. On the next screen, click the small arrow next to **Disk drives** to reveal your laptop's hard drive details. Today's laptops have SATA (serial ATA) hard drives, which use small USB-like connectors for data and power

3 Check with your laptop manufacturer, or visit one of the reputable online shopping sites that allow you to select the make and model of your laptop and see which hard disks are compatible

laptops & netbooks

Upgrade your hard disk

1 Rather than re-installing the operating system and applications, and restoring all your files (such as music, photos and video) to the new drive, you can use disk-cloning software to recreate your old hard drive's contents. Simply dragging-and-dropping the contents from one drive to another will not work. There are several free Windows utilities that clone hard drives, including EASEUS Disk Copy and Clonezilla, but paid-for clone software can be a better choice for those who are not computer experts

2 To clone your old hard drive you need to connect the new hard drive to your laptop. This can be done using a USB-to-SATA adaptor cable, which costs around £15 from computer retailers and online stores such as Amazon

3 Once the drive is connected, and your chosen clone software program has launched, follow the on-screen instructions to copy your old hard drive. Be aware that cloning operations can take a long time so set aside plenty of time

4 When cloning is completed, unhook the new hard drive and turn off and unplug the laptop

5 How you access the hard drive in your laptop will vary by manufacturer and model type, but usually it involves removing a set of screws that secure a compartment door on the bottom of the laptop. The compartment door then slides or lifts up

6 The hard drive usually sits in a caddy from which it needs to be unscrewed. Undo these screws and remove the old hard disk

7 Place the new hard disk in the caddy and replace the screws

8 Slide the caddy back into the laptop and secure the compartment

9 Turn the laptop over and power it up. The system should reboot as normal, but from the new drive, with all your applications and files ready for use

TRY THIS

If you prefer not to root around inside your laptop, consider an external hard disk drive that connects to your laptop via the USB or FireWire ports. Although these drives may hinder the portability of the laptop, they're a cheaper solution and let you upgrade to a much larger capacity.

▶ Laptops & Netbooks

Upgrade your laptop battery

Laptops use rechargeable batteries so they can be used when not connected to the mains. The performance of laptop batteries does degrade after some time, depending on the amount of use. Follow the tips on page 26 to get the most from your laptop's battery, but if the performance remains poor you can upgrade to a new battery. Here's how:

1 Turn off your laptop and disconnect all cables

2 Release the latch on the compartment on the bottom of your laptop that holds the battery in place

3 Slide the old battery out of its storage bay

4 Slide the replacement battery into the bay

5 Close the safety latch and lock it into place

6 Plug in the mains adapter and give the battery a full charge

WATCH OUT!
You may wish to upgrade the graphics performance of your laptop, but as most laptops come with an integrated graphics chip built into the motherboard, this is near impossible. Some high-end laptops do offer this facility, but it is a difficult and time-consuming process that's best left to a specialist computer technician.

TABLET PCs

By reading and following all the steps in this chapter, you will get to grips with:

- **Choosing the right tablet PC for you**

- **Essential features and connectivity**

- **Setting up your tablet PC**

# Tablet PCs

TABLET COMPUTERS EXPLAINED

Tablet PCs – also known as media tablets – are best described as portable, touchscreen, internet-connected computers, which operate in a similar way to large smartphones (see Smartphones chapter, page 131). They differ from laptops by having no physical keyboard, being a lot less powerful, and by generally being simpler to use and operate.

Tablets are primarily designed for interactive entertainment, such as listening to music, watching movies, reading ebooks, playing games, or using the web. Apple's iPad was the first tablet to gain mainstream popularity, and a range of tablets that broadly offer similar features are now on sale.

Tablets can also be used for productive applications, such as word processing and photo editing. If you want to use a tablet for work, a model running Windows will allow access to standard office suites, while the iPad can be used with Apple's iWork software. There is a variety of software available for all tablets and for many tasks – from music creation to business applications.

Advantages of tablets

- ▶ Lighter than laptops, making them easier to carry and lighter to hold and use – especially for long periods of time
- ▶ Touchscreen interface offers more natural use and simpler navigation – for example, a gesture made on the screen, such as a finger swipe, will scroll through text
- ▶ The range of software is generally excellent – with hundreds of thousands of programs, called 'apps', available that perform most tasks, such as word processing, spreadsheets and photography
- ▶ Quick to use – tablets switch on and are ready to use instantly, without the waiting time it takes to switch on a laptop
- ▶ Digital creativity – such as digital painting – is more intuitive using a tablet due to its flat, interactive surface
- ▶ Easier to learn – operating systems on tablets are simpler than those on laptops, and direct on-screen manipulation of applications make them easier to control and use
- ▶ Additional features – many tablets include features such as GPS (the location technology found in sat-nav devices) which help to find your location on a map, digital compasses, and the ability to automatically rotate the screen to match the tablet's orientation
- ▶ Battery life – tablets are designed with portability in mind, and battery life is typically around ten hours of continuous use

Disadvantages of tablets
▶ Expensive – compared with a laptop, tablet computers cost significantly more, with prices ranging from £250 to £600, depending on the model. There are very cheap tablets on sale for less, but these are best avoided due to poor performance
▶ Lower performance – tablets are powered by low-power processors, making them unsuitable for demanding activities such as video editing and visually rich video games
▶ Screen damage – as it lacks a lid, the screen of a tablet computer is exposed to higher risk of damage, such as scratches
▶ Lack of keyboard – an on-screen keyboard tends to be slower at entering text than a physical keyboard, and the flat screen of the tablet makes it difficult to position so you can rest your wrists.

Why do I need a tablet?

Tablets offer the ideal combination of portability and practicality, but if you've already got a laptop or netbook and a smartphone, there's little more you can do with a tablet. One of the best features of tablets, however, is that they are fast to switch on, and ideal for occasional web browsing, rather than waiting for a full PC to start up.

They're slimmer and lighter than netbooks, and smaller tablets can be comfortably held in one hand for reasonable periods of time.

Most tablets offer all the features of a touchscreen mobile phone, but in a larger size. A 7- or 10in (17.75- or 25.5cm) screen makes them more suitable for web browsing, watching videos and reading ebooks than the 3–4in (7.5–10cm) screens on smartphones such as the Apple iPhone.

The additional screen space means that on-screen keyboards are more usable, although for prolonged typing you're better using a physical keyboard. Many tablets can connect to physical keyboards, and these are sold as optional extras.

OPERATING SYSTEMS

One of the first decisions to make when choosing the best media tablet, is the operating system. Media tablets generally follow the same basic user interface design: a series of 'homescreens', similar to computer desktops, with shortcut icons and menus that are used to access applications, or 'apps'. See page 34 for an explanation of computer interfaces.

iOS

The iPad runs Apple's iOS operating system: a simple, intuitive interface that also gives access to the Apple App Store. iOS can run multiple applications at the same time – called multi-tasking. Apple's iPad iOS, however, won't play the Flash content used for many videos you can watch online, so the websites you view in Apple's Safari browser will have gaps where Flash content should be.

Android

Most tablets run variations of Google's Android operating system, which was originally designed for smartphones. Tablet manufacturers are able to customize this software to suit their own specifications, enabling them to get the best out of it for their devices. This can be a weakness, with multiple versions of Android meaning that some apps only work on the latest version of Android, which might not be the one included on your tablet.

Tablets running Android seamlessly integrate with users' Google accounts for email, documents, contacts and maps. Unlike Apple iOS, Android can play Flash in web browsers and apps.

It's important to check reviews of Android tablets; some of the cheaper ones can be quite poorly made, and lack the features and usability of premium Android tablets.

Windows 7

Although Windows is primarily designed for PCs with keyboards, some media tablets run Microsoft Windows 7 via their touchscreens. The advantages of a Windows tablet PC is that it is similar to the version that runs on PCs, so many people are already familiar with it, and the vast array of compatible software. Windows does tend to require a higher-specification tablet, which will therefore be more expensive, especially when the cost of the Windows software licence is included. (See page 88.)

BlackBerry tablets

BlackBerry's PlayBook runs the company's own operating system, is Flash-compatible, and offers many of the business-oriented features that make BlackBerry smartphones so popular.

Dual-boot tablets

The final option is to pick a 'dual-boot' tablet – a device that can run more than one operating system – usually Windows and Android. These tablets give you the flexibility of using a full-featured operating system (OS) such as Windows 7 for running desktop applications such as full web browsers, office suites and other software, while also running the lightweight Android OS for apps.

TABLET FEATURES

Tablet specifications

Tablets, being mini touchscreen computers, share many of the components of their more complex relatives such as laptops. Processors – the microchips that power them – range from around 1GHz upwards, with the faster ones giving more power and speed of operation, as well as less chance of slowing down when performing processor-intensive tasks such as watching HD video.

Tablet app stores

Key to the tablet experience is the ability to customise them with additional apps – software programs that include word processors, ebook readers, games, finance software and more. Apple's iPad connects to the Apple App Store, which offers the widest range of apps, and also features digital versions of many popular magazines.

Google's Android Market for Android-based tablets is a close second for the variety of apps and games available. However, due to its smartphone heritage, Android only allows devices that can connect via 3G access (see page 174) to the Android Market app store. This rules out many of the cheaper tablets that only have Wi-Fi. As an alternative, these tablets feature their own proprietary cut-down app stores. If you're looking for the full Android experience, with access to more than 100,000 apps, then the meagre alternatives offered by most Android tablets are likely to leave you disappointed.

Touchscreens
Tablet touchscreens, as with mobile phones, come in two types – resistive and capacitive – with capacitive screens generally being more responsive, and also more expensive.

Tablet screens vary in size, currently from the 7in (17.75cm) screen on the Samsung Galaxy Tab, to around 10in (25.5cm) on the iPad. Larger screens are more useful for sharing between people, for example during multiplayer games. A 10in (25.5cm) screen also gives plenty of room for an on-screen touch keyboard. Tablet size and weight varies considerably, depending on whether the tablet's casings are made from metal and glass, or plastic, which is found on cheaper media tablets.

Jargon buster

Resistive and capacitive touchscreens
Both technologies allow you to use a computer or mobile device by touching the screen. Resistive touchscreens use pressure from a finger or stylus. Capacitive touchscreens use your own finger's electrical properties to detect when and where the display is being touched.

⊳ Tablet PCs

Multi-touch screens, such as that on the Apple iPad, allow several fingertips to be registered by the screen at one time. This allows the on-screen display to be manipulated intuitively, such as 'pinch to zoom', where a pinching action between two fingers on a screen will zoom out from a photo or map.

With touchscreens, screen reflectivity and fingerprints are important to consider. If you're planning to use your media tablet outside, choose a less reflective screen that will be better in bright sunlight. To reduce fingerprints, the iPad has a grease-resistant oleophobic coating.

It's also worth checking the screen resolution and aspect ratio – Samsung's Galaxy Tab has a resolution of 1,024 x 600 pixels and a 16:9 screen – ideal for watching widescreen videos, whereas the iPad has a resolution of 1,024 x 768 in a 4:3 aspect ratio – more suited to web pages, ebooks and digital magazines. More pixels mean more detail, and higher pixel densities (pixels per inch) give a sharper image.

Connections

Most tablets connect to a PC or Mac via USB, either by a proprietary connector such as those found on the iPad and Galaxy Tab, or by using a standard mini or micro USB socket.

They usually come with a fixed amount of built-in memory, too. Typically you get either 16GB or 32GB, but some can have additional memory added via memory card slots, taking either SD or microSD cards. Some cheaper tablets feature just 8GB of on-board memory, not leaving much space to store apps, photos and video.

Tablets are ideal for watching videos on the move, but some also have outputs for connection to a TV. The best solution is an HDMI output socket (see page 44), but some tablets, including the iPad, require an adaptor to connect to a VGA socket on a TV or monitor. A 3.5mm (0.8in) headphone socket, for headphones, speakers or a hi-fi, is standard on tablets.

3G, Wi-Fi, Bluetooth and GPS

For connecting to the internet, some tablets have 3G connectivity so they can use mobile phone networks for data as well as calling and texting. These media tablets have slots for either a standard SIM card, or for smaller microSIMs. As with smartphones, 3G media tablets are available either on Pay-As-You-Go (PAYG) or on monthly contracts, with different levels of monthly data allowance.

You can connect hands-free Bluetooth headsets to tablets for making telephone calls, so you don't have to hold a large device to your ear to use it as a phone.

GPS is a feature on all but the most budget media tablets, so they can also be used for location-aware services, maps, and as large-screen, in-car sat-navs.

▶ Tablet PCs

ADDITIONAL FEATURES

Cameras

Some tablets have one or more built-in cameras – either on the rear so they can be used as a very large touchscreen camera, or on the front for video-calling.

However, camera resolution is generally low, so tablets aren't designed to replace your compact camera or camcorder. For example, a tablet might have a 3Mp camera on the rear, and a 1Mp camera on the front, which are low quality compared with the resolution found on the latest digital compact cameras. Better tablets feature LED flashes and more advanced camera features such as panoramic photos and smile detection. Some tablet cameras can record video, although generally at a low resolution.

Music and video

All media tablets allow the playback of music and video files, but check compatibility with the types of files you will want to play. The best media tablets will handle a variety of standards, including Mpeg4, WMV, H264 and DivX video files and MP3, AAC, WMA, Flac and Wav files.

The iPad ties you to using iTunes software to manage your media. In contrast, many other tablets can be connected to PCs and Macs via USB where they appear as separate storage drives, so files can be dragged and dropped on to them. All tablets feature synchronising software to help managing media files across your devices.

Battery life

Lack of stamina is a major issue for tablets. Apple's claimed battery life for the iPad is 10 hours, but in real-world use the battery lasts for closer to eight hours. Watching videos or browsing the web are likely to drain the battery even faster. Smaller tablets can have an even shorter battery life – the Samsung Galaxy Tab averages around four hours of use, and some cheaper tablets struggle to last half that time.

And if you're thinking of using a tablet for reading ebooks, be aware that it won't offer anywhere near the battery life of a dedicated ebook reader such as Amazon's Kindle. Tablet PCs use LCD screens, rather than the e-ink screens of ebook readers. E-ink screens only use energy from the battery when you turn a page, whereas back-lit LCD screens require constant energy to display each page of text. Furthermore, the e-ink screens on ebook readers are designed to make reading more comfortable, resulting in less eyestrain.

Tablet accessories

Tablets such as the iPad and Galaxy Tab have a range of optional accessories make them easier to use, transport and to add new features. Accessories include cases and sleeves to protect them while on the move (see page 209).

A useful accessory is a media dock, stand or keyboard dock that enables the tablet to be supported at an angle similar to a computer monitor, with a keyboard providing a more ergonomic typing solution compared to the on-screen keyboards. Docks can also operate as chargers for your media tablet; in-car chargers are also available.

APPLE IPAD EXPLAINED

The Apple iPad is a portable digital entertainment device with a large 9.7in (24.5cm) touchscreen that lets you access the web, write emails, flick through photos, watch films, view maps, and even type word documents using its 'virtual' on-screen keyboard.

WATCH OUT!
The iPad is powered by a special chip created by Apple called the A4 processor. It runs at 1GHz, and iPads come with 256MB of Ram. It is impossible to add more Ram or a faster processor, or even change the battery.

Similar to an oversized iPhone, it has a high-resolution LED multi-touch screen in a light case that weighs 680g (1.5lb) – around the weight of a paperback book. Just 1.25cm (0.5in) thick, it has a battery that will last up to ten hours while surfing the web, watching a video or listening to music. It works in both portrait and landscape orientations, with the screen automatically rotating as the device is turned.

The iPad is controlled using your fingers with swipes, gestures and taps on the screen – allowing you to visit web pages, write a document or find your location using Google Maps.

It can connect to home and public Wi-Fi networks, and works with Bluetooth devices such as wireless headphones. An optional 3G model will connect to mobile broadband, although you'll need to pay an extra, on-going cost to use mobile broadband through a mobile phone network, such as O2.

The iPad includes up to 64GB of storage, a built-in speaker and microphone, and a special connector for attaching a keyboard and recharging. Some models include GPS and a digital compass. The iPad does just about everything you could want from a portable entertainment and media tablet.

Apple iPad features

Apple's iPad has lots of apps for everyday tasks such as surfing the web, photos, email and video.

Photos Flick, pinch and tap your way through your entire photo collection with ease. Albums are shown as stacks of photos that, when tapped, open to show all the photos within. Photos can be shown full-size, and when you rotate the iPad over to show off a photo, the photo rotates too. The iPad also has a Faces feature – just tap someone's face to see all the photos of that person.

Photos can be added by syncing the iPad to a Mac or PC using iTunes (see page 193), or you can add them from a camera or SD card. You'll need to buy the optional iPad Camera Connection Kit for this, however.

WATCH OUT!
The iPad does not support Flash technology – which means it won't play back some video found on the web, nor interactive Flash games. However, it does mean you don't get to see Flash-based ads on web pages.

Video Video is shown in high definition, and, as there are no control buttons, you get a full-screen viewing experience. Films and TV programmes can be rented or purchased directly from the iPad – although the screen size means that widescreen movies don't use the entire screen, with black borders appearing top and bottom. YouTube videos can be viewed, and you can share YouTube favourites with friends using email, or by posting the video onto Facebook.

Internet Apple iPad includes the Safari web browser, and can show entire web pages in both portrait and landscape mode. Web surfing is controlled with your finger: flicking pages to scroll up and down, and double-tapping to zoom in or out. Active web pages can be viewed in a gallery so you can jump directly to them, and pages are visited when a link to that page is touched.

Maps You can view searchable, high-resolution satellite images of the world, as well as routing and directions. It is also possible to zoom into a map until you are virtually standing in a street using Street View.

Email The iPad includes an on-screen keyboard for composing email messages, with large keys and the ability to suggest words, correct spelling and insert punctuation as you type. Typing on a glass screen, however, feels quite different to using a physical keyboard. Email shows both the messages in your email inbox, and a view of the opened email. Email can include photos, as well as Microsoft Word, Excel, PowerPoint and PDF files. Emailed photos can be added to the iPad photo library with a single tap.

iPod Access and play your music collection, browsing by song, artist, album and genre. Albums can be flicked through using your finger, and songs synced with iTunes on a Mac or PC.

Notes Use the virtual keyboard to jot down notes and to-do lists. Notes can be saved, edited and emailed to friends, or saved to a desk or laptop computer.

Calendar Appearing as a paper-style, day-to-view desk calendar, the Calendar app can create different calendars such as work and home. These calendars can be synchronised across computers and online services such as Google Calendar.

Contacts Like a digital version of a leather-bound address book, Contacts can also include photographs, the ability to tap a contact and email them directly, and set calendar reminders. Tap an address, and the location is shown in the Maps app.

iBooks for the iPad This turns the iPad into a full-colour ebook reader. Its touchscreen interface let you turn pages using your fingers, and you can alter the type and size for easier reading. The iPad can access a digital ebook online store for buying and downloading books directly on to the iPad, with many bestsellers and popular books available to buy, as well as providing free books, including classics such as *Alice In Wonderland.*

Tablet PCs

APPLE IPAD OPERATING SYSTEM

Unlike a traditional laptop or desktop computer, the Apple iPad runs a different operating system to Microsoft Windows or even Apple's own Mac OS X. Instead, it runs a system called iOS, which Apple created specially to run on its portable devices such as the iPad, iPod Touch MP3 player, and iPhone mobile phone.

Interface

Apple's iOS is designed to be operated by fingers instead of a mouse, which means it recognises gestures such as touch, swipes, flicks and pinch-and-drag to control the on-screen interface (see page 34).

The interface isn't like a traditional PC desktop – it lacks waste bins and menus. Instead, each application is shown on the iOS desktop as a tile – when tapped, the application will run. Pressing the 'home' button will take you back to the desktop so you can use another application.

Like on a PC, you can change the background image, drag applications to new areas, group them together, and adjust settings such as time, date, and internet access information.

Multi-tasking

The latest version of the iOS operating system allows for multi-tasking on the iPad. This means the iPad can run several applications, such as a web browser and word processor, at the same time, and switch between them instantly.

Applications

Because the iPad lacks a DVD or CD drive, all software has to be purchased through the Apple-run App Store. You need to set up an iTunes account first (see page 101) and pay by debit or credit card, then download your chosen application onto the iPad, or on to your PC and then transfer it to your iPad.

Apple claims there are hundreds of thousands of applications on its App Store, and there are applications for nearly every use – from photo editing and music creation, to office software and games. Prices are very low – ranging from free to around £5.99 depending on the software.

Accessibility

The iOS used on the iPad includes many built-in accessibility options, including screen-reading technology, which allows those who have poor vision to hear a description of the item they're touching on the screen. The iPad also has dynamic-screen magnification, white-on-black text, and playback of closed-captioned video, and you can use more than 30 different wireless Braille displays with it.

Security

Unlike a desktop PC, the Apple iPad is very secure and free from viruses. Because software can only be installed from Apple's App Store, and because of the structure of the iOS, you don't need to install anti-virus security software on the iPad.

Other iOS 4.2 features

The iPad's operating system includes the basic features that you'd expect to find on a laptop, including the ability to print – but only to printers connected to a Wi-Fi network – spell checking across all documents, global search, the ability to organise applications into folders, and security features such as password settings.

Upgrading

Apple uses its iTunes software on Mac and Windows PCs to download and sync apps to the iPad – although you can download apps directly to the iPad itself. Software upgrades – which are provided free by Apple – require the iPad to be connected to a Mac or Windows PC running iTunes. The upgrade will download, then install automatically on to the iPad.

Tablet PCs

GOOGLE ANDROID TABLET PCS EXPLAINED

Most tablet PCs in stores are based on Google's Android operating system – a mobile interface for controlling tablets that uses a touchscreen in the same manner as Apple's iPad. Unlike the iPad, which is only available from Apple and runs the iOS operating system, Android tablets are made by a number of different companies, including Toshiba, Samsung, and even UK retailer Next.

Android features

Much like the Apple iPad, Android tablets have a set of features for viewing photos, websites, video and ebooks – but there are some features that differ.

Google apps Google Android tablets include a range of Google applications designed to be productive, help you find your way, and watch video. The applications included do vary by manufacturer and tablet device, so check first before buying. Typical applications broadly available across all Android tablets include:

Gmail An email application that uses Google's web-based email service. Emails sent to Gmail automatically appear when they arrive on the tablet, and you can search through previous emails.

Google Maps Full access to Google's excellent mapping service, including the ability to search your local area, plan routes, and find out where you are. If the tablet includes a GPS chip, then it can work like a sat-nav, giving turn-by-turn directions to your destination.

YouTube As well as playing video stored on the tablet, Android tablets can play video from YouTube, much in the same way as the iPad can. You can also upload video taken with an Android tablet to YouTube to share it with others.

Google Calendar This allows you to store dates and events, then sync them with an online version of Google Calendar, so you stay up-to-date across a range of devices, not just your tablet PC.

Other Google Apps Depending on the tablet, Android devices include applications for storing contacts, using spreadsheets and word processing, instant messaging, and Google Chrome for surfing the web.

Hardware Because Android tablets are made by a range of companies, specifications and hardware vary dramatically. Screen sizes can range from 5–10in (12.75–25.5cm) or more, run on different processors, and come with a range of storage sizes – from 2GB to 64GB. However, some features separate Android tablet hardware from that of the Apple iPad.

Expansion Android tablets typically offer more expansion and upgrade options than an iPad, including memory card slots for increasing storage, and USB ports for connecting devices such as digital cameras.

Voice calls Many of the more expensive Android tablets include the ability to make voice calls using the tablet, much like a mobile phone. You'll need a contract with a mobile phone operator to use this feature.

Cameras Most Android tablets include digital cameras – usually a lower-resolution camera on the front for video conferencing, and a slightly higher-quality camera on the back for taking photos and recording video. Video is recorded in standard-definition quality, much the same as UK terrestrial television.

Memory Memory affects the number of programs you can run at the same time, and how successfully the tablet can handle more complex tasks such as video editing. Memory varies by tablet, but ranges from 128MB to 512MB.

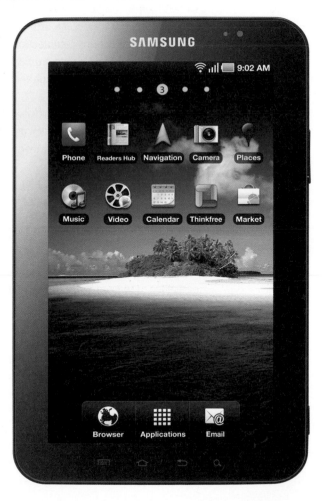

Tablet PCs

ANDROID TABLET OPERATING SYSTEM

Much like the iPad's iOS operating system, Android is a specially created mobile operating system originally designed for smartphones. It was created by Google – the internet search engine – and the company has made it freely available to other manufacturers to use on smartphones and tablets.

Unlike Apple's iOS, however, Google Android wasn't designed specifically for tablet devices, which can lead to some compatibility problems. For instance, unless the tablet includes 3G wireless mobile broadband, the tablet may not be able to access Google's Android Market to browse, buy and download apps – software programs – to run on the tablet.

Interface

Google Android tablets can be controlled using fingers, rather than a keyboard and mouse, and support a range of gestures such as swiping, flicking and dragging elements around the screen. Numerous homescreens – equivalent to a PC's desktop screen – can be set up, with a finger swipe moving between each screen. Apps can be dragged into position on the screen, such as clocks and weather forecasts, and more complex apps – such as word processing – launched with the tap of a finger.

Like on a laptop, you can change the images on the homescreens, as well as adjust settings and set up internet access. Android features a virtual, on-screen keyboard for entering text.

Each manufacturer can create its own, redesigned version of the Android operating system, adding extra functionality and features, as well as a unique look and feel for each tablet model.

Multi-tasking and Flash

Android is capable of running several apps at the same time, and can also display Flash content. Flash is a type of content that powers many videos and interactive games on the web, although Flash performance can be a bit slow and drain the battery of the tablet faster.

Applications

Android tablets do not have optical drives so you can't install applications directly from a CD. Instead, Android features the Android Market – similar to the App Store found on the iPad and iPhone. This is a collection of lots of different types of applications – from general everyday computing such as finance software and photo-editing tools, to games and interactive books.

However, Android Market does not have as many apps as Apple's App Store and, because of restrictions, Android Market is not available on tablets unless they have a wireless 3G mobile broadband connection. This means cheaper Android tablets don't include access to the Market, making it difficult to add programs to them.

Security

Due to its infancy, there have been few security threats to Android, and the closed nature of the tablet means that it doesn't suffer from viruses and trojan malware in the same way that a laptop or desktop PC does, so you don't need to install separate anti-virus software.

Other features

Android includes the basic features that you'd expect to find on a laptop, including spellchecking across all documents, global search, the ability to organise applications into folders, and security features such as password settings.

Upgrading

Google regularly releases new versions of its Android operating system, adding new features. However, due to the fragmented nature of the Android tablet market, not all tablets can be upgraded to the latest version. Before buying, check with the manufacturer that the tablet will be able to upgrade to newer versions of Android as they become available. Unlike the iPad, Android can be updated directly onto the tablet itself, without requiring it to be connected to a PC.

Jargon buster

Trojan
A trojan is a type of computer virus. It is disguised as an innocent program to encourage people to install it. A trojan allows third parties remote yet complete access to your computer files.

Jargon buster

Malware
Malware is a generic term used to refer to any piece of malicious software that will harm your computer, such as a virus.

▶ Tablet PCs

WINDOWS TABLET PCS EXPLAINED

Microsoft has enabled its Windows operating system to work on tablet PCs since the release of Windows XP in October 2001. Its latest version – Windows 7 – has a range of features designed to work on tablet PCs, such as support for touchscreen interfaces, handwriting recognition, an on-screen keyboard, and the ability to use a stylus to enter text and control the screen.

Unlike both iOS and Android, Windows 7 for tablet PCs is a fully fledged operating system that works in the same way as it does on laptops or desktop PCs. Windows tablet PCs are available from PC makers – typically Dell, Samsung and HP – and these are often more powerful tablets than those running iOS or Android. Because Windows 7 tablets are effectively keyboard-less laptops, you can do everything you'd be able to on a laptop, including editing video, surfing the web, email, playing games, and editing photos.

Tablet PC specifications
As Windows 7 tablet PCs are created by a range of different companies, specifications differ between tablets.

Windows 7 tablet PC processors
Unlike the iPad, Windows 7 tablets use processors typically found in netbooks and laptops from Intel or AMD. These are lightweight, low-powered processors designed for general computing, such as the Intel Atom, and can be up to 2GHz in speed.

Memory, storage and screens
In line with other tablets, Windows tablets use solid-state storage disks – typically with 64GB of storage space. Memory is, however, far higher as Windows 7 is a demanding operating system when it comes to memory needs. Windows tablets usually have up to 2GB of memory, around eight times that of the original iPad. However, that memory is necessary as Windows 7 was designed as a laptop and desktop operating system.

Screen sizes differ dramatically, but are around the 9in (23cm) mark. Screens are multi-touch, but many use a resistive screen technology rather than capacitive (see page 73). The advantage of this is that you can use a stylus to prod buttons and write text, but using fingertips to control the on-screen action can be sluggish.

Connections, ports and expansion

Windows 7 tablets offer lots of expansion options, including USB ports for connecting other devices such as printers and cameras. Most Windows 7 tablets include at least one, and usually two, USB ports. Windows 7 tablets also include expansion card slots – usually for SD or microSD media cards – to expand the storage space of the device. All Windows 7 tablets include Wi-Fi wireless access, as well as Bluetooth for controlling the screen with a physical keyboard and even a mouse.

Tablet PCs running Windows 7 also usually include a camera or two – one on the front for video conferencing, and one on the rear for taking photos and video. Video can often be output to a TV using a HDMI cable connection.

Finally, many Windows tablet PCs, such as the HP Slate 500, include a dock and stylus for charging the device and connecting other devices. The stylus can be used for handwriting input, as well as for controlling menus and dialog boxes.

▶ Tablet PCs

WINDOWS TABLET PCS OPERATING SYSTEM

The Windows 7 operating system (see page 88) which runs on tablet PCs is the same Microsoft system that runs on Windows laptops and desktop PCs. It features the exact same interface – including folders, software applications, desktop icons, taskbar and Windows 7 Start menu. The desktop can be fully customised – such as changing the background wallpaper – and it gives the same level of control over settings.

Because it is a fully fledged version of Windows 7, you can download, install and run any software that Windows 7 supports – including Microsoft Office, games, photo-editing software such as Windows Live Photo Gallery, email and any web browser, such as Internet Explorer or Firefox. Software can't be installed from a DVD however, as Windows tablets lack an optical drive.

If you have used a Windows desktop PC or laptop, you'll be instantly familiar with the interface and all your software will work with a Windows 7 tablet.

Windows 7 tablet features
As well as delivering the Windows 7 desktop in a tablet form, Microsoft has added a handful of features to Windows 7 specially designed for tablets. Features include virtual on-screen keyboards, support for touch controls, and both handwriting and maths recognition software.

Handwriting support

As Windows 7 tablets mainly use a stylus for control, the handwriting recognition feature means that the tablet can interpret an individual's handwriting in a broad range of languages. You can also create a custom dictionary for specialised vocabulary such as medical terms, for example. Text prediction is available to help speed up note-taking.

Maths support

A new feature in Windows 7, the Math Input Panel can recognise shapes and symbols, allowing you to write mathematical equations or chemical formulae directly on to the screen using the stylus. These equations and formulae can then be copied into any application that accepts MathML (Mathematical Markup Language), such as Microsoft Word.

Touch and go

You can control the tablet using fingertips. Gestures mimic the activities for which you'd use a mouse – for example, touching and holding down on an icon is the same as right-clicking it with a mouse, and calls-up a pop-up menu. Flicking a web page or open document will scroll it, while touching with two fingers and rotating will turn an object, such as an image.

Tablet PCs

HOW TO CHOOSE THE RIGHT TABLET FOR YOU

With so many tablets available – from Apple iPads to the numerous Android and Windows 7 tablets – choosing the right tablet PC for you can be a challenge.

Here is a guide to some of the things to consider when choosing your tablet.

Size

Tablets come in a variety of sizes – from the 5in (12.75cm) Dell Streak to the 9.7in (24.5cm) iPad, and a range of sizes in between. Larger screens are more useful when watching video, surfing the web, reading a digital book or magazine, and for sitting on the sofa at home and using it.

Larger screens, however, mean heavier tablets, and while the 9.7in (24.5cm) iPad can be lugged around in a bag or rucksack, it won't fit into a purse or small bag. If portability is important, then a 7in (17.75cm) tablet – such as the Samsung Galaxy Tab – might appeal. Overall, it is roughly half the size of an iPad, but, due to the smaller screen, controlling applications can be fiddly.

Battery life

Tablets are designed to be portable and used without being plugged in to a power source. Most tablets will offer three to five hours of battery life when being used to play a movie – although Apple's iPad has space in its larger frame to house more battery capacity, lasting up to ten hours before it needs to be recharged.

All tablets can be recharged by connecting them to the mains, or to the USB port of a laptop or desktop PC. Think about how often you will need to recharge your tablet when weighing up which one is right for you.

Which operating system?

Operating systems are a matter of personal choice, but with three different versions available, choosing the right one can be hard.

iOS Apple's iOS is available only on one tablet PC – the iPad. As a dedicated mobile operating system, iOS has also been on the market the longest, has plenty of features, and is quick and surprisingly powerful. It was designed specifically for the iPad and iPhone, and has access to Apple's App Store with over 40,000 iPad apps. Choose iOS for the biggest range of software, as well as its ease of use and simplicity.

Apple's iOS, however, won't play Adobe Flash content which is used for video and animation on many websites, so your online browsing experience may be affected. Also iOS is available only on Apple products and it's not as customizable as Google Android.

Android is the best choice if you want a tablet other than an iPad, but need similar functionality. Not as mature as iOS, Android is more customisable, upgraded more frequently, and has lots of features that appeal to more advanced computer users.

However, because each manufacturer uses its own version of Android, the Android tablet market is fragmented – not all apps will work on all tablets. Android does have its own app store, but many tablets don't include access to it, limiting their appeal.

Windows 7 gives you the full functionality of a laptop in a tablet form. It will be compatible with your software and ways of working if you already use Microsoft Windows 7, but will also have the same pitfalls around security and viruses.

Windows 7 wasn't designed specially for tablets – and trying to press menus and use a desktop operating system controlled with your fingers can be slow, fiddly and awkward. Windows 7 tablets also tend to be the more expensive of the three systems.

Finger control or stylus?
Stylus or finger? Multi-touch or single touch? Tablets offer a range of options to control the screen, with the camps broadly split into stylus control or fingertip control.

Choose a stylus if handwriting input is vital, and you're happy to use a stylus to select items on the screen. A stylus is usually limited to a single touchpoint to interact with on-screen content, much like the cursor of a mouse.

Choose fingertip multi-touch to get the best tablet PC interactivity. It might be a new way of controlling a computer, but fingertip control supports gestures and gives an immediacy with the content you are controlling. Using on-screen keyboards is easier with fingertips than with a stylus.

▶ Tablet PCs

WATCH OUT!

Apple's iPad requires a powered USB port to charge, which can rule out using older PCs to charge it up. Luckily it comes with a mains power plug to charge it as well.

Wireless Wi-Fi or 3G?

Tablets cost less if you choose a Wi-Fi only version, but while tablets that also include 3G mobile broadband cost more, their purchase price can be discounted if bought as part of a mobile broadband contract.

Choose Wi-Fi if you don't plan to access email and the web when on the move, and will mainly be using your tablet at home with a home Wi-Fi connection. If you do go out and about, you'll be able to use Wi-Fi hotspots – many for free – in railway stations, cafés and airports. You'll also benefit from a cheaper purchase price.

Choose 3G if you're happy to sign up to a mobile broadband contract for 18 months or more as this can lower the purchase price of a tablet. Choose this option if you need to access the internet from any location in the UK – even when away from Wi-Fi hotspots – for basic web surfing and email. You'll also get Wi-Fi access included in the price.

What's best for applications?

As tablet software applications can only be bought using the devices from online stores, tablets do vary in the range and number of software programs – called 'apps' – that they feature.

Choose iPad and iOS if you want the broadest range of apps. At the time of writing, Apple has over 40,000 dedicated apps for iPad, and more than 250,000 apps that work on both the iPhone and iPad. The quality varies, but high-quality word processors, spreadsheets, games, music creation tools and productivity apps are either free or typically cost between £0.59 to £5.99 each.

Choose Android if you want access to apps in the same way as Apple's App store. However, the Android Market has far fewer apps than Apple, and the quality varies even more dramatically.

Choose Windows 7 if you want to run Windows 7 software, such as Microsoft Office. You can run commercial software, but it typically costs much more than apps from an app store, and some software needs to be installed from a DVD drive, which Windows tablet PCs lack.

What do you want to do with it?
The ultimate decision on which tablet is right for you depends on what
you want to use it for.

For entertainment choose an iPad. With its big screen, access to iTunes,
thousands of downloadable entertainment apps, and the ability to view
high definition video, the iPad is a great entertainment device. Even
better, it has access to the iBooks store to download the latest books, and
provides a great reading experience with its long-lasting battery.

For productivity choose Windows 7, especially if you work in business
and need access to lots of Windows 7 software. Arguably, all tablets can
be productive, but Windows 7 tablets have the edge – albeit for a cost
and weight penalty.

For customisation choose Android tablets, which offer a far-ranging
degree of control (such as using a different web browser) and also
a range of different sizes and features to better match your needs.

Pricing
How much you want to pay for a tablet depends on your budget, but our
advice is to avoid cheaper tablets. These are often underpowered, have
limited access to download other applications, and feature poor screens
that will leave you feeling frustrated. Good quality tablets typically start
from around £400.

▶ Tablet PCs

TRY THIS

The set-up process for a Windows-based tablet PC is similar to setting up a Windows laptop. See page 48 for details on setting up a laptop.

SETTING UP A TABLET PC

Tablet PCs are easier to set up and get running than laptops and desktop PCs, and set up is usually similar to setting up a smartphone (see page 166). Each type of tablet is different, however, and some – such as the Apple iPad – must be connected to a Windows or Mac computer as part of the set-up process.

Setting up an iPad

1 Download and install iTunes, and create an iTunes account (see page 101 for details on doing this) on your computer. Once installed, take your iPad out of the box, and plug the accompanying cable into the dock connector at the base of the iPad, and plug the other end into a USB port on the computer that is running iTunes

2 On the screen that appears on your computer, click **Continue** to register your iPad. On the following screen, agree to the terms and conditions, then click **Continue**

3 On the following screen, ensure that **Use my Apple ID to register my iPad** is checked (your Apple ID is set up as part of the iTunes account creation process detailed in step 1), and enter your Apple ID, then click **Continue**

4 Over the following few screens, enter your registration details, decide whether to take up a free MobileMe trial (Apple's email and calendar service – this is not essential). Choose **Set up as a new iPad** on the following screen, then click **Continue**

5 On the following screen, give the iPad a name (such as Which iPad), and choose if you want to automatically sync songs and videos, photos and applications you have added to iTunes to your iPad. You can change these settings later. When the set-up is done – click **Apply** to begin syncing your music, photos, videos and applications to the iPad

Connecting to a Wi-Fi network

To access email and the web, as well as download apps directly to the iPad, you'll need to set up a connection to your home Wi-Fi network.

From the Home Screen, tap **Settings**, then tap **Network** and then **Wi-Fi**. Ensure Wi-Fi is toggled **On**, then tap on a Wi-Fi network name. Enter the password, then tap **Save**.

iPad settings

When you've set up your iPad, you can change some of the settings depending on how you want the iPad to operate. Tap the **Settings** icon to access all the settings for your iPad – from connecting to a wireless network (see page 50) to setting passcodes (see page 104). Here are some of the changes you can make:

Brightness & Wallpaper This adjusts the screen brightness, and you can set automatic brightness control. You can also choose a photo from photos synced to the iPad as wallpaper.

Safari This allows you to customise the Safari web browser, such as blocking pop-up ads and choosing the default search engine, such as Google.

General This controls sounds, language, date and time, and any parental restrictions you might want to apply.

Setting up an Android tablet

As Android-based tablets are made by a variety of different companies, set-up can vary between tablets. Here we've used the Archos 101 Internet Tablet as an example.

1 Take the Android-powered tablet from the box, and fully charge the battery before use following the instructions in the manual. Once charged, unplug it and press the power button

2 The Installation Wizard will run. Follow the on-screen instructions, setting the language, time and country for the tablet

3 To transfer songs and videos to the Android tablet, find the USB cable, and connect one end to the tablet, and the other to a Mac or Windows computer. When the tablet asks if you want to connect it, press **Mount** on the tablet screen. After a few moments, the tablet will appear as an icon on your computer desktop

4 To transfer files, such as music and photos, drag them onto the tablet icon on the desktop, copying them into the relevant folders on the tablet. Once done, on a PC click **safely remove hardware** from the System Tray next to the clock. On a Mac, drag the tablet icon to the trash can. You can now unplug the tablet

Connecting to a Wi-Fi network

You can connect your tablet to a Wi-Fi network to access the internet and download applications on to the tablet.

1 From the **Home Screen**, tap **Settings**, then tap **Wireless & networks**, then tap **Wi-Fi** settings

2 The tablet should automatically detect all available Wi-Fi networks. Locate your Wi-Fi network from the list, and tap it

3 Enter the password for the network, then tap **Connect**. The tablet will connect to the Wi-Fi network ready to access the internet

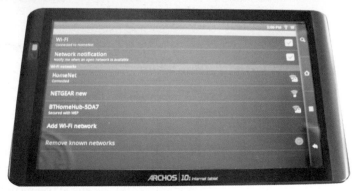

Android tablet settings

From the Home Screen, tap the Settings button to gain control of key settings for the tablet.

Sound & Display is used to adjust audio settings, media volume, and display settings such as animation, brightness, and orientation.

Date & Time allows you to set the date and time. You can also set the tablet to automatically update time and date settings when it is connected to the internet.

Language & keyboard sets options for the on-screen keyboard, and allows you to add and remove words from the user dictionary.

TABLET APPLICATIONS

Unlike laptops and desktop computers, most new tablet PCs lack an optical disc drive, such as a DVD or CD drive, to install applications. Also, you cannot buy applications on the high street as you can with boxed PC software. Instead, tablets use online stores – the App Store for the iPad and Android Market for tablet PCs that run the Google Android operating system.

These 'app stores' host tens of thousands of applications designed to work on tablet PCs, and applications can be downloaded over a broadband connection directly to the tablet and installed. Apps can also be downloaded on to a laptop or PC connected to the app store, then transferred – called 'syncing' – by attaching the tablet to the USB port of the laptop or desktop PC.

To purchase an app from an app store, you'll need to install special software, such as Apple iTunes, on your computer, and register a credit or debit card with the store. Alternatively, access to app stores is usually available directly from the tablet itself.

Set up an Apple iPad and App Store using a Windows PC
While you can directly access the App Store from an Apple iPad, accessing, purchasing and downloading apps for the iPad using a laptop or PC is preferable. PCs have more space to store apps, you can select which ones to transfer to your iPad, and you have a handy backup of purchased apps if you accidentally delete one from your iPad.

Additionally, you can transfer apps from a laptop or desktop PC to as

many iPads as you want to associate with your App Store account.

Mac OS X users already have iTunes installed by default, so can skip to Setting up an iTunes account.

Download iTunes

1 Using a Web browser, visit www. apple.com/uk/itunes/ and click the blue **Download Now** button

2 The iTunes download page should automatically pick the correct version of iTunes for your PC operating system, such as Windows. If you want, untick to opt out of the marketing offers. Once done, click **Download Now**

3 In the dialog box that appears, click **Run**. Once the download has completed, click **Run** again in the new dialog box that appears

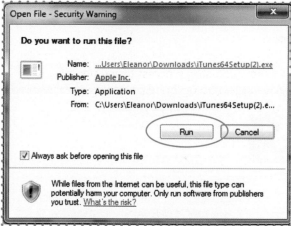

4 Follow the installation instructions to install iTunes on your Windows PC

Set up an iTunes account

1 Launch iTunes by clicking on the iTunes program icon, then choose **Create Account** from the iTunes Store menu and follow the on-screen instructions.

You'll need to enter a valid credit or debit card to purchase items from the iTunes store, which includes the App Store

Using the App Store

1 Click the iTunes program icon to launch iTunes, and make sure that you are connected to the internet. In the main window, click **iTunes Store** in the left-hand navigation panel. The iTunes Store will load, showing music and videos that you can download to your iPad

2 Click App Store in the top, black menu bar across the top of the iTunes Store. This will show the front of the App Store, and showcase a collection of new and noteworthy applications to download. You can toggle between iPhone and iPad apps – click the iPad button in the centre top of the App Store screen

3 To view different app categories – such as games, business or music apps – click-and-hold the App Store menu and choose the category of app you want

4 To view an app, click the app icon or name. This will show images of what the app looks like and give a description of the app. Scroll down the page to read reviews from other purchasers to see how good it is

5 To buy an app, click **Buy App**. Confirm you want to purchase it, and the download will begin. Downloaded and purchased apps are added to the Apps section of iTunes, accessed by clicking **Apps** in the left-hand navigation panel

Syncing apps with an iPad

1 Plug the USB cable that came with the iPad into the base of the iPad and, with iTunes running on your computer, plug the other end into the desktop or laptop PC

2 Your iPad will appear listed in the left-hand navigation panel of iTunes, and syncing will begin automatically. iTunes will install all downloaded apps, as well as any music and videos you may have purchased, on to the iPad

3 To select the apps you want to install – rather than install all of them – wait for the iPad sync to finish, then click your iPad icon in the left-hand panel of iTunes. Select **Apps** in the top menu, then untick the apps you don't want to install

4 Press **Sync Now** to add the selected apps to the iPad. Once the sync is complete, click the small eject icon next to the iPad icon in the left-hand panel of iTunes. Unplug the iPad from the USB cable, and you are ready to use the apps you have added

ANDROID MARKET

The Android Market – available on some Android tablets – works on a similar principle, but access varies between tablets. Check the manual for your tablet for details on how to use the Market to download apps.

▶ Tablet PCs

TABLET SECURITY

The small size and portability of tablet PCs makes them easy to carry around in a more casual way than, say, a laptop. It also means they are more vulnerable to being misplaced or stolen.

While there are plenty of practical steps to keep your device safe from theft (see page 205), there are also some things you can do to secure the personal information stored on the tablet PC itself.

Privacy settings may also be useful if, for example, the tablet is used by the whole family and you wish to restrict access to age-relevant apps or videos.

Whichever tablet you use, you can find security settings by accessing the device's **Settings** menu from its home page. In this example we have used Apple's iPad.

Passcode (password) and screen lock

Set up a strong passcode lock for your iPad as this will prevent someone from accessing your personal data without your permission. It also makes it less attractive to thieves as it can't be re-synced to a new computer without this code.

Set a passcode

1 Select **Settings**, then tap **General**, then tap **Passcode Lock**

2 Enter a four-digit passcode, then enter the passcode again to verify it

The iPad will now require you to enter the passcode to unlock it or to display the passcode lock settings.

Turn the passcode off

1 Select **Settings**, then tap **General**, then tap **Passcode Lock** and enter your passcode

2 Tap **Turn Passcode Off**, then enter your passcode again

Change the passcode

1 Select **Settings**, then tap **General**, then tap **Passcode Lock**, enter your passcode

2 Tap. Enter your passcode again, then enter and re-enter your new passcode

Set a period of time for auto-lock

Choose how long the iPad remains inactive before it is automatically locked. To reactivate the device you will then need to type in the passcode.

1 Choose **Settings**, then tap **General**, then tap **Passcode Lock**

2 Enter your passcode. Tap **Require Passcode**

3 From the list, tap to select how long iPad can be idle before you need to enter a passcode to unlock it

Turn on the Erase Data function

This function will wipe all the personal information and media on your iPad should someone make ten consecutive incorrect passcode attempts. Be careful, if this happens all your settings are then reset to their original values and all your data will be lost.

1 Select **Settings**, then tap **General**, then tap **Passcode Lock**

2 Enter your passcode

3 Tap **Erase Data** to turn it on

Remote tracking and locking

Apple allows you to remotely locate a missing iPad using its free Find My iPad service – and you can also lock it and remotely wipe the data from the iPad.

1 To use this, you'll need to download the free Find My iPhone app from the App Store – this works for Apple iPhones, iPads and the iPod Touch – and have access to a computer

WATCH OUT!
The iPad's default mode lets anyone view your photographs, even if it's locked, by clicking the flower icon so make sure your photographs are suitable for general viewing.

2 On the iPad tap the **Settings** menu, then tap **Mail, Contacts, Calendars**

3 Tap **Add Account**, and tap **MobileMe**

4 Enter your Apple ID (this is the same as your iTunes account) or tap **Create Free Apple ID** and follow the instructions

5 Once verified, switch on **Find My iPad**

6 Using a computer, you can now see your iPad on a map when you log into the MobileMe service from Apple

Restrictions

If your iPad is used by the whole family, you may want to limit access to apps, disallow app installation, and set age restrictions for access to, for example, explicit music or YouTube.

Turn on restrictions

1 Choose **General**, then tap **Restrictions**, then tap **Enable Restrictions**

2 Enter your passcode

3 Re-enter the passcode

Set application restrictions

Set the restrictions you want by tapping individual controls on or off. Initially, all controls are on (unrestricted). Tap an item to turn it off and restrict its use.

Set content restrictions

If you tap **Ratings For,** you can set restrictions using a particular country's entertainment ratings system for categories of content that include music, movies and television shows. Here, we've selected the UK for its familiar rating system.

EBOOK READERS

By reading and following all the steps in this chapter, you will get to grips with:

- Which ebook reader to choose

- Setting up your ebook reader

- Buying and downloading ebooks

EBOOKS AND EBOOK READERS EXPLAINED

Ebooks are electronic books, where the text and pictures of a printed book have been digitised into an electronic format.

Ebooks can be read on computers, such as laptops and netbooks, many mobile phones and on dedicated devices which are generally called ebook readers.

The beauty of most ebook readers is that they are as light as a paperback and as slim as a magazine. And they allow you to carry thousands of ebooks, magazines or newspapers in one easy-to-use handheld device. This, combined with their long battery life, makes them a perfect travelling companion and an alternative to a groaning bookshelf at home.

Unlike smartphones, laptops and netbooks which tend to have glossy colour LCD (liquid crystal display) screens, dedicated ebook readers use a different screen technology that makes them easier to use for reading ebooks.

They use an 'electronic ink' display – a matt grey-on-grey screen designed to be more easy on the eye. These screens are easier to read in direct sunlight and from different angles than regular LCD screens, so you won't suffer from eye fatigue.

With many ebook readers now featuring wireless or 3G connection to the internet, you can buy and download books direct to the reader itself rather than doing it via a computer. Alternatively, you can load pre-purchased books or documents from your computer, then transfer them to your ebook reader using a cable.

The number of ebook readers available is mushrooming, with more technology companies such as Sony, as well as booksellers such as Barnes & Noble, and Amazon, releasing models. Prices vary from as little as around £100 to £400 or more.

Advantages of ebooks

Ebooks have several advantages over a printed book:

▶ As the file size of an ebook is small, the internal memory of most ebook readers can store thousands of ebooks. Some devices can also use external memory cards so that even more ebooks can be stored

- Unlike a printed book, ebook type is flexible. Most ebook readers allow you to alter how you view an ebook, with options to change the typeface, font size and orientation of the text. Any ebook can therefore become a large-print book, which is great for those who struggle to read small print

- Bookmarks and auto-resume functions mean you can easily find your place after you've taken a break from reading an ebook

- You can easily search an ebook for a particular word or phrase using the device's search function

- Ebooks can be cross-referenced using hyperlinks

- Many ebooks are free. All fiction published before 1900 is in the public domain and so, if it's available, it can be free to download

- Some ebook readers allow you to share a copy of an ebook with another person for a limited time

- You can download ebooks from your local library – they will be automatically deleted from your device when the loan period is up, saving you the trouble of physically returning a book

Disadvantages of ebooks
- If your ebook reader battery runs out, or you are away from a mains supply, you won't be able to read your ebook

- Some ebooks, particularly new releases, are no cheaper to buy than the printed versions

Jargon buster

Hyperlink
A hyperlink is text or an image that, when clicked, allows you jump to another web page when surfing the internet or, in the case of ebooks, takes you to another linked page.

Ebook Readers

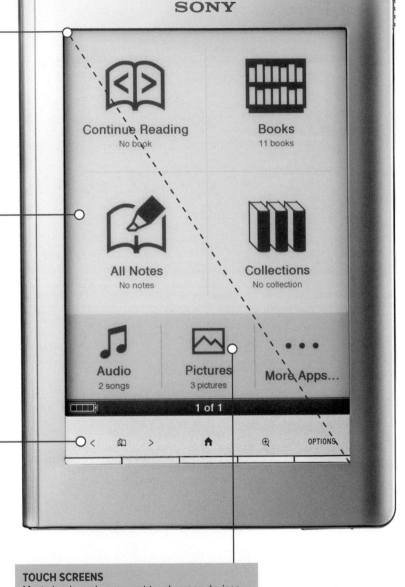

SCREEN
As with laptops, an ebook reader's screen size is measured across the diagonal of the screen. Ebook readers' screen sizes range from a tiny 5in (12.75cm) to nearly 10in (25.5cm).

SCREEN TYPE
Unlike laptops, which use backlit LCD screens, ebook readers use electronic ink or e-ink displays. The advantages of an e-ink screen are paper-like readability, that can be viewed under different light conditions including direct sunlight, and low power consumption, which means that a battery charge lasts for a long time.

CONTROLS
Controls vary between ebook readers, but most feature prominent buttons for turning the pages of a book, as well as navigation buttons for looking at the library of titles stored on the reader. Other controls include volume and power buttons.

TOUCH SCREENS
Most ebook readers are not touchscreen devices, relying on hardware buttons to turn pages. A few do feature touchscreens, allowing you to add notes, look up words and flick through the pages.

WIRELESS CONNECTIONS
Most ebook readers feature a Wi-Fi connection for linking to home networks and downloading books. A few have 3G mobile broadband for browsing and buying books while out and about.

PORTS
Ebook readers have a limited range of ports – typically a USB port for syncing to a computer, a headphone socket, and a power-charging port. Built-in speakers and a headphone port mean you can listen to audiobooks. If the ebook reader includes an MP3 player you will be able to listen to music too.

KEYPAD
Some ebook readers have a qwerty keypad, which can be used to perform keyword searches and edit filenames and directories.

EBOOK READERS FEATURES

On the face of it, ebook readers lack the simplicity of a traditional book. But the best ebook readers are compact, straightforward to use, and have many user-friendly features.

Screen size

Ebook readers come in a range of screen sizes. A 6in (15cm) screen is typical, but larger models, such as Amazon's Kindle DX, will have a screen of up to 10in (25.5cm).

Larger screens make it easier to read text, but it means that the device itself has to be bigger – so don't expect to fit a large ebook reader into a pocket. Smaller screens make for a pocket-sized device, but you may need to zoom in on a page to read the text.

Electronic ink

Ebook reader screens look different to normal backlit displays (such as LCD screens, which are used on laptops and smartphones).

This is because they use an 'electronic ink' (or e-ink) display – a matt grey-on-grey display that's easy to read, even in bright sunlight and from many different angles. These electronic ink displays also use a fraction of the battery power used by the power-hungry LCD screens featured on laptops, tablet PCs and smartphones. The device uses no power to actually display a static image such as a page of text or a menu; power is only required to change the screen, for example when you turn a page.

Text wrapping

Oliver Twist

and a rub alternately. As the young woman spoke, he rose, and advancing to the bed's head, said, with more kindness than might have been expected of him:

'Oh, you must not talk about dying yet.'

'Lor bless her dear heart, no!' interposed the nurse, hastily depositing in her pocket a green glass bottle, the contents of which she had been tasting in a corner with evident satisfaction.

'Lor bless her dear heart, when she has lived as long as I have, sir,

1%   Locations 23-26   5973

Oliver Twist

and a rub alternately. As the young woman spoke, he rose, and advancing to the bed's head, said, with more kindness than might have been expected of him:

'Oh, you must not talk about dying yet.'

'Lor bless her dear heart, no!' interposed the nurse, hastily depositing in her pocket a green glass bottle, the contents of which she had been tasting in a corner with evident satisfaction.

'Lor bless her dear heart, when she has lived as long as I have, sir, and had thirteen children of her own, and all on 'em dead except two, and them in the wurkus with me, she'll know better than to take on in that way, bless her dear heart! Think what it is to be a mother, there's a dear young lamb do.'

Apparently this consolatory perspective of a mother's prospects failed in producing its due effect. The patient shook her head, and stretched out her hand towards the child.

The surgeon deposited it in her arms. She imprinted her cold white lips passionately on its forehead; passed her hands over her face; gazed wildly round; shuddered; fell back—and died. They chafed her breast, hands, and temples; but the blood had stopped forever. They talked of hope and comfort. They had been strangers too long.

'It's all over, Mrs. Thingummy!' said the surgeon at last.

'Ah, poor dear, so it is!' said the nurse, picking up the cork of the green bottle, which had fallen out on the pillow, as she stooped to take up the child. 'Poor dear!'

'You needn't mind sending up to me, if the child cries, nurse,' said the surgeon, putting on his gloves with great deliberation. 'It's very likely it will be troublesome. Give it a little gruel if it is.' He

1%   Locations 23-34   5973

Ebook readers can wrap or re-flow text, which means that the text size and display should change to fit the screen of the particular device you're using, regardless of its screen size or your individual settings. So, for example, if you increase the font size, the text will rearrange itself so that you can continue to read as normal, without having to scroll from left to right.

Screen rotation

If you prefer to hold your ebook reader in a horizontal position, some readers allow you to rotate the screen so that the text can be read in this way.

Oliver Twist   Wi-Fi .ıll 🔋

and a rub alternately. As the young woman spoke, he rose, and advancing to the bed's head, said, with more kindness than might have been expected of him:

'Oh, you must not talk about dying yet.'

'Lor bless her dear heart, no!' interposed the nurse, hastily depositing in her pocket a green glass bottle, the contents of which she had been tasting in a corner with evident satisfaction.

'Lor bless her dear heart, when she has lived as

1%   Locations 23-26   5973

Touchscreens

Some ebook readers have a touch-sensitive screen. This can be used to activate different functions by tapping different areas of the screen, or to turn pages with a sweep of a finger.

Touchscreen ebooks may also have a stylus or electronic pen to allow you to select and annotate text.

Page 1 of 1

Text-to-speech function

Some ebook readers include text-to-speech software that converts words on the screen into digitally synthesised speech, which can be heard through the reader's speakers or by using headphones.

For many people, text-to-speech is simply a fun gimmick, but if you struggle to read print, it can be an essential way to access a book.

Unlike a performed audiobook, which includes the emotion and pace of an author's work, text-to-speech can sound stilted and mechanical. On the plus side, this can allow you to draw your own interpretations from the text.

Dictionaries

A handy feature when reading an ebook is access to a dictionary, and many ebook readers feature built-in dictionaries. Amazon's Kindle includes two – The New Oxford American Dictionary (which is the default dictionary) and the Oxford Dictionary of English.

With the Kindle, for example, you can look up a particular word without leaving the ebook page. Using the controller, simply place the cursor in front of the word in question. A definition of the word then appears at the top or bottom of the screen. For a fuller definition, press the Return key on the keyboard. When finished, press the Back button to return to the text you were reading.

Headphones

Most ebook readers will have a headphone socket. This gives you the opportunity to listen to audio books (.aa and .aax files) or text-to-speech functions with some privacy.

Many ebook readers can play digital music (MP3) files too, so you can listen to music while reading an ebook.

Controls

Most ebook readers will have specific buttons for carrying out the most common tasks – turning a page, for instance. And you'll usually find a small joystick or directional keys for navigating through menus.

If you buy an ebook reader with a built-in keyboard, such as the Amazon Kindle, you'll be able to use this to enter text – for example, to search for specific terms within an ebook or dictionary.

However, keyboards do take up quite a bit of space at the bottom of the ebook reader, reducing the space available for the screen itself.

CONNECTIVITY FEATURES

USB port

Your ebook reader will have a USB connection and you'll probably also find a USB cable in the box it was supplied in. This will let you connect your ebook reader to your PC or laptop, so you can load it with downloaded ebooks and recharge it at the same time.

Some ebook readers cut out the need for a USB connection to a computer and allow you to connect to the internet wirelessly and download ebooks straight to the reader.

SD card slot and SD card

On average, ebook readers can store almost 2,500 ebooks. If you want more storage space, look for a reader with a memory card slot that can take a memory card such as an SD card. This will boost the storage capability of your ebook reader dramatically.

Before you buy a memory card for your ebook reader, check in the user manual what type of memory card it supports.

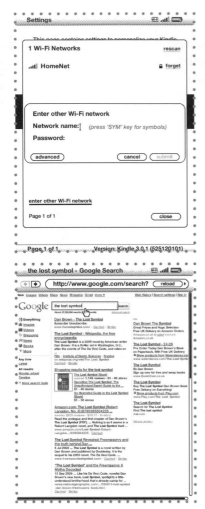

Wireless connections

Some ebook readers are able to download content wirelessly, using the same 3G network as a mobile phone.

This makes it easy to choose and purchase new ebooks, or even daily content such as news, but it will have an impact on the device's battery life – usually making it shorter than that of ebook readers that connect to a computer.

The Amazon Kindle DX, for example, has free Wi-Fi and 3G connectivity – Amazon's 3G Whispernet network – so there are no monthly fees for connecting to the Kindle store (although fees may be incurred if used outside the UK).

With the Kindle DX, Amazon is experimenting with some new features including a basic web browser that allows you to surf the internet through a Wi-Fi hotspot only (3G connectivity is limited to accessing the Kindle store). You can access this by pressing the **Menu** button from the **Home** page and scrolling down until **Experimental** is underlined, and then pressing the central button of the navigation controller to select. Remember that you will see web pages in black and white only.

Battery life

Charging an ebook reader is simple. Most will charge via a USB cable when connected to your computer, but if you prefer, you can use a mains charger instead.

The battery life of ebook readers is generally impressive as the electronic ink screen draws no power when static. Power is only used when you 'turn' an electronic page. Most manufacturers claim that you'll get between 6,000 and 8,000 page turns before you need to recharge – a figure that would get you through the complete works of Shakespeare several times over.

However, ebook readers that use wireless connections, such as the Amazon Kindle, can consume more power. You can expect to get one to two weeks of use from a Kindle before you need to recharge.

CHOOSING THE RIGHT ONE FOR YOU

With so many features and factors to consider, choosing the best ebook reader for you isn't a simple task. Pick the right ebook reader and it will prove an ideal companion that will provide many hours of reading enjoyment. Make the wrong choice, and you could be faced with just as many hours of frustration.

To help you with your decision, here's a list of the most important factors to consider:

File format

This should really be your starting point when considering which ebook reader to buy. Check which file formats your ebook reader supports. Consider whether you intend to read only ebooks. If you want to display images, play audio books or MP3 files, or even subscribe to RSS feeds (see page 156) and magazines, then carefully check the file formats supported by your chosen device.

The number and type of ebooks available

Next, visit the online bookstore for the reader you're considering and check that the titles you want to read are available in the correct file format. There's no point buying an expensive reader only to find that the books you want to read aren't available in the format supported by that device.

Kindle ebook readers, for example, can only get ebooks from Amazon. However, as Amazon is the biggest retailer of ebooks, this shouldn't be too much of a disadvantage.

Connectivity

Another factor that can help narrow down your choice is connectivity. To access an ebook on your ebook reader, you must first download the book to your computer before transferring it to your reader through a USB cable.

However, if downloading books directly to your reader is important to you, choose a model with a built-in wireless connection. The Amazon Kindle, for example, provides wireless connection to download ebooks along with basic internet browsing.

Jargon buster

MP3 file
MP3 is the standard file format for digital music. It is a popular format because it is not tied to one manufacturer, unlike Apple's AAC and Microsoft's WMA files.

Ebook Readers

Storage capacity
The storage capacity of ebook readers varies across models and manufacturers. Less expensive ebook readers may only store a few hundred books, while the Amazon Kindle DX can store a whopping 3,500 books. If you need even more storage, consider an ebook reader with a memory card slot.

Screen size and weight
Size matters – especially if you want to your ebook reader to be really portable. Ebook readers come in a wide range of sizes, from Sony's Reader Pocket with its 5in (12.75cm) screen, which can fit into your jeans' pocket, right up to large devices such as the Kindle DX that sport screens of about 10in (25.5cm) in size.

While smaller ebook readers are easier to carry around, those with larger screens are better for people with poorer eyesight because you can make the font much larger. If you have trouble reading the normal text size of a paper book, you may choose a model that lets you adjust the onscreen text size.

Along with the screen size, consider the quality of the text displayed. Most ebook readers offer a greyscale display, although many manufacturers are now developing colour screen readers.

Screen displays are rated in levels of greyscale. A cheap ebook reader may feature a four-level greyscale display, while a higher-end model has up to 16 levels of greyscale. A higher greyscale level means crisper text and a better reading experience.

Battery life
Battery life will only be a consideration if you plan to travel with your ebook reader. As long as it will last for two or more weeks, then you should be fine. But remember that devices with Wi-Fi and web browsing will tend to have shorter battery life.

Price
As with most consumer electronic devices, the more you spend, the wider range of features you will get with your ebook reader. However, there are plenty of mid-price ranged ebook readers that will satisfy the needs of an avid reader.

SETTING UP AN EBOOK READER

Once you've purchased your ebook reader, setting it up is simple. This example uses an Amazon Kindle, but setting up other types of ebook reader will require a similar procedure that includes registering for a store account and downloading reader software.

First, you will need an amazon.co.uk account to purchase and download content for your Kindle. Once this has been created, you can then register your Kindle to this account.

1 On the Kindle Home screen, press the **Menu** button and select **Turn Wireless On**

2 Press the **Menu** button and then use the controller to scroll down through the options until **Settings** is underlined, then press the central button of the controller to select

TRY THIS
If you have a Wi-Fi-only device, you will need to set up your Wi-Fi connection in order to register from the ebook reader itself. See page 127 for how to set up a wireless connection on a Kindle.

ebook readers

▶ Ebook Readers

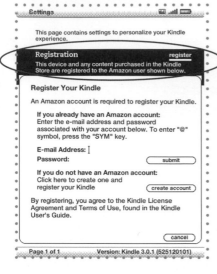

3 Press the controller to select **Register** from the Settings screen

4 Enter your amazon.co.uk user name and password (the email address and password associated with your Amazon account) using the keyboard. If your Amazon user name or password contains numbers or characters not present on the Kindle keyboard, press the **Symbol** key (SYM) to see a menu of additional characters

5 Using the navigation controller select **Submit** to finish the process

Set up your payment method

When you buy ebooks, or other content, directly from your Kindle, you pay using the default 1-Click payment method available on your amazon.co.uk account. This is usually the payment method associated with your default delivery address.

For digital purchases, you can use a credit or debit card or amazon.co.uk gift certificates.

Check or change your payment method

1 Visit the **Manage Your Kindle** page on Amazon's website

2 Click the **Your 1-Click payment method** link in the shortcuts box on the right-hand side of the page

3 Click **Edit** to change your payment method, then follow the on-screen instructions for choosing or adding a payment method

Set a password

To make sure only you and authorised users have access to your Kindle, you can set a password. This means that you will have to enter the password to access your Kindle if it enters sleep mode or is turned off.

1 Navigate to the **Home** screen and press the **Menu** button

2 Select **Settings**

3 Select **turn on** option next to **Set Password** on Settings page

4 Enter your new password twice and a hInt to help you remember it

5 When you have finished select **Submit**

If you wish to change or turn off your password, navigate to the **Settings** menu again and select from the available options.

TRY THIS

If you forget the password to your Amazon Kindle, move the controller down to view your password hint. Your Kindle will also give you a phone number for the Kindle support team who can help you to reset your Kindle password.

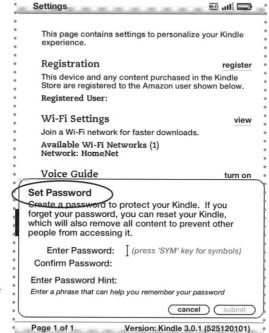

Settings

This page contains settings to personalize your Kindle experience.

Registration   register
This device and any content purchased in the Kindle Store are registered to the Amazon user shown below.
Registered User:

Wi-Fi Settings   view
Join a Wi-Fi network for faster downloads.
Available Wi-Fi Networks (1)
Network: HomeNet

Voice Guide   turn on

Set Password
Create a password to protect your Kindle. If you forget your password, you can reset your Kindle, which will also remove all content to prevent other people from accessing it.

Enter Password: [*(press 'SYM' key for symbols)*
Confirm Password:

Enter Password Hint:
Enter a phrase that can help you remember your password

cancel   submit

Page 1 of 1   Version: Kindle 3.0.1 (525120101)

▶ Ebook Readers

Contents

Cover
Title
Copyright
Dedication

Chapter One
Chapter Two
Chapter Three
Chapter Four
Chapter Five
Chapter Six
Chapter Seven
Chapter Eight
Chapter Nine
Chapter Ten
Chapter Eleven
Chapter Twelve
Chapter Thirteen
Chapter Fourteen
Chapter Fifteen
Chapter Sixteen
Chapter Seventeen
Chapter Eighteen
Chapter Nineteen
Chapter Twenty
Chapter Twenty-One
Chapter Twenty-Two

1%   Locations 4-33   1

Ebook structure

Once you have downloaded an ebook (see pages 126 and 127), when you view it on an ebook reader, the structure will be the same as the printed version of the book. For example, if the book has a table of contents, this will appear in Kindle. So too will chapters, the preface and an illustrated cover, if they exist in the printed version.

Each page of the ebook will display a header showing the content title and/or issue date.

Set text size, words per line and screen rotation

You can choose from eight different font sizes to find a text size you can read comfortably – the text size menu, however, is fixed and cannot be altered. Kindle ebook readers also let you change your screen rotation and set the number of words per line.

WATCH OUT!
You cannot change the number of words per line in PDF files or in web text.

Change your text formatting options

1 Press the **Text** key on the keyboard (the button with a large and small capital A on it) to display the text size menu

2 Move the controller to set the size of text and typeface you prefer

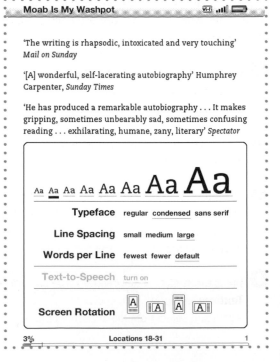

Moab Is My Washpot   Wi-Fi ▪▪▪▪▌ 🔋

'The writing is rhapsodic, intoxicated and very touching'
Mail on Sunday

'[A] wonderful, self-lacerating autobiography' Humphrey Carpenter, *Sunday Times*

'He has produced a remarkable autobiography . . . It makes gripping, sometimes unbearably sad, sometimes confusing reading . . . exhilarating, humane, zany, literary' *Spectator*

Aa A̱a Aa Aa Aa Aa Aa Aa

Typeface   regular condensed sans serif

Line Spacing   small medium large

Words per Line fewest fewer default

Text-to-Speech   turn on

Screen Rotation 🄰 🄰 🄰 🄰

3%   Locations 18-31   1

Change the line spacing

You can adjust the space between lines of text. Well-spaced lines of text are easier to read than densely packed blocks of text.

1 Press the **Text** key located on the bottom row of the keyboard. The **Line Spacing** choices of small, medium and large are displayed below the text size choices

2 Move the controller down to underline the **Line Spacing** option

3 Move the controller left or right to choose the option you want to use. The text on screen will change immediately so you can see the effect of your changes

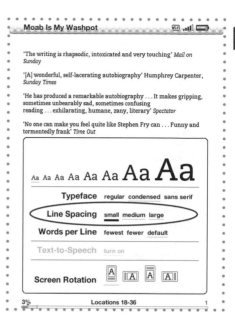

Change the number of words per line

You can adjust the number of words per line displayed in the ebook to suit your reading preference. Fewer words per line may help you to read faster. Changing the number of words will increase or decrease the size of the margins.

1 Press the **Text** key located on the bottom row of the keyboard. The **Words per Line** choices are displayed below the text size choices

2 Move the controller down to underline the **Words per Line** option

3 Move the controller left or right to choose the option you want to use. The text on screen will change immediately so you can see the effect of your changes

4 Press the central button of the controller or the **Text** key to confirm your choice

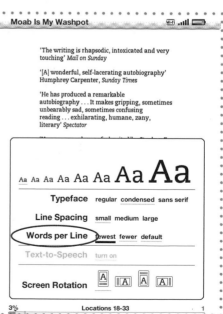

EBOOK FORMATS

Ebooks come in various file formats, and not all ebook readers are compatible with all types, so check carefully which one your ebook reader will support before you buy or start downloading ebooks online.

New ebooks are copy-protected, restricting the number and type of devices they can be read on, but older ebooks (notably those out of copyright) tend to be available free in unprotected file formats.

ePub format

One of the most common ebook file formats available is the ePub standard – a popular open standard created by the International Digital Publishing Forum. Most ebook readers, apart from the Kindle, work with the ePub format. EPub books are available from most ebook reader independent stores.

AZW format

This is the format that Amazon Kindle uses, and the majority of books on the Kindle store are available in this format.

BBeB/LRF Sony Reader format

Sony ebook readers use this format – although Sony ebook readers also support the ePub standard.

Adobe PDF

Adobe Acrobat PDF documents are commonly used for free content. Usually the electronic version looks just like the print version. PDFs work on most ebook readers but tend not to display as tidily as ePubs when using the zoom or reflow options.

Digital Rights Management issues

DRM, or Digital Rights Management, is designed to combat piracy and places restrictions on what you can do with your electronic books.

For example, a book from Amazon will be in the AZW format and will only work on Amazon Kindle ebook readers.

Some ePub books are unprotected and can be used on any device, but those entitled 'Adobe ePub' are protected with DRM from Adobe. This means you can use the ebooks on up to six devices (including the computer used for downloading).

Jargon buster

Digital Rights Management
DRM is a system for protecting the copyright of digital content (such as music, books, images and video) that is distributed online, whether it is downloaded, printed, or viewed, or shared across computers and other devices.

EBOOK STORES

Many ebooks cost less than printed versions of the same book, but new releases will be similarly priced.

If you're not looking for the latest bestsellers, there are thousands of free public domain ebooks online. Once the UK copyright in all elements of a book has expired (including all content, illustrations and other copyright rights) it can be distributed electronically for free within the UK.

Project Gutenberg (www.gutenberg.org), an online library stacked with 30,000 free titles, is a good place to start. Another place to look is Google Books.

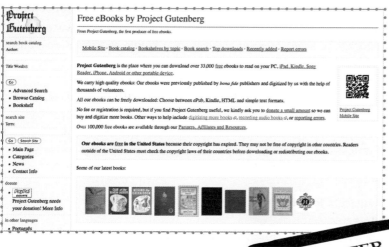

Good sites for buying ebooks

▶ Amazon Kindle Store (www.amazon.co.uk)
▶ Waterstone's (www.waterstones.com)
▶ Kobo Books (www.kobobooks.com)
▶ Booksonboard.com (www.booksonboard.com)
▶ Borders (www.borders.com)
▶ WHSmith (www.whsmith.co.uk)
▶ MyBeBook.com (http://mybebook.com)
▶ Penguin eBooks (www.penguin.co.uk)

BUY AND DOWNLOAD AN EBOOK

Buying and downloading an ebook is fast, convenient and, with no costs for postage and packing, can be great value. Ebooks can be downloaded in seconds.

Whichever online store you choose to buy from, you'll need to set up an account and enter your payment details first. Then, it's simply a question of choosing an ebook and following the on-screen instructions to purchase and download the title. In this example, we have used the Amazon Kindle store which offers all types of content, including ebooks for Kindle ebook readers.

Connecting to the Kindle Store
If you're buying ebooks using your PC or Mac, simply type **www.amazon. co.uk** into your web browser and then click **Kindle** and then **Kindle Store** from the left-hand menu on the home page.

However, if your Kindle ebook reader has 3G connectivity and you're in an area where Amazon's Whispernet coverage is available, you can directly access the Kindle Store on your Kindle. This allows you to buy and download Kindle books, newspapers, magazines and blogs wirelessly, using your Kindle.

Connect to the Kindle Store on your Kindle

1 If Whispernet is not already on, press the **Menu** button and select **Turn Wireless On** using the controller

2 Check your connection by checking the connection status indicator in the upper right-hand corner of the Kindle screen

3 Press **Menu** button and select **Shop in Kindle Store**

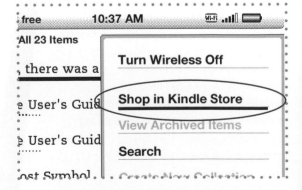

Navigating the store using your Kindle

Once your Kindle is connected to the Kindle Store, there are many ways to find ebooks. The opening menu displays the following options:

▶ **Browse the Kindle Store** shows the content available in the Kindle Store by type. Categories include books, magazines, newspapers and blogs

▶ **Kindle Bestsellers** lists the store's bestselling titles

▶ **New & Noteworthy Books** lists new or noteworthy books

▶ **Kindle Post** links to a blog from Amazon on content-related topics

▶ **Editors' Picks** show recommended ebooks

Once you've clicked a category from this list, you can refine your browsing by topic. For example, within **Books**, you can look at listings for **Fiction**, and **Nonfiction**.

To quickly find an ebook, enter keywords such as author or title into the **Search** box at the bottom of every page.

Once you have selected a title, the product detail page will be displayed. This shows a range of useful information about that particular ebook, including author name, story description, and customer reviews. You can add the title to your Amazon Wish List to purchase later, see what other customers who bought this book also bought, and download the beginning of the book for free so that you can sample it before buying.

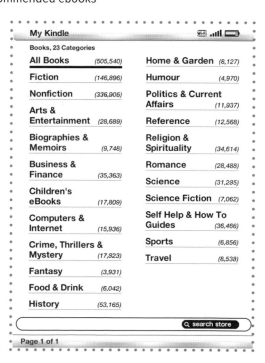

Ebook Readers

TRY THIS

To retrace your steps while browsing the store on your Amazon Kindle, scroll to the top of the current page and select a category from the browse path to return to that section. You can also use the Back button to return to previously browsed pages.

When you're ready, click the **Buy** button to purchase the ebook using your default 1-Click payment method. This is automatically enabled after you've placed your first order with amazon.co.uk.

The ebook will then be sent wirelessly to your Kindle for free, usually within 60 seconds. Press the **Home** key to see your purchase in the list of titles.

If it's not there, open the **Home** menu and select **Check for New Items**. If the item is not listed, check your **Show and Sort** options at the top of the screen. You can also check your delivery status on the **Manage Your Kindle** page on Amazon's website.

Download an ebook to your computer

You can also download direct to your computer and transfer it via USB to your Kindle. To do this, simply type **www.amazon.co.uk** into your web browser and then click **Kindle** and then **Kindle Store** from the left-hand menu on the home page. Navigate to the product detail page (or the Manage Your Kindle page).

1 On the product detail page, click **Deliver to:** and from the pull-down menu select **Transfer via Computer**

2 Save the file to your computer

3 Connect Kindle to your computer with the USB cable

4 Locate your new ebook using your computer's file browser, then drag and drop the file to your Kindle's **Documents** folder

ALTERNATIVES TO EBOOK READERS

Ebook readers are great devices but, for some people, you can't beat the simplicity of a traditional paper book. They're easy to use, cheap, and able to survive impacts without damage.

What's more, an ebook reader is another expensive accessory that risks being stolen or damaged when you're travelling.

Aside from the obvious alternative of traditional paper books, there are other options that are well worth a look.

You can read ebooks on laptops, smartphones and tablet PCs. Some ebook reader publishers have created special 'apps' to allow their ebooks to be read on these devices. For example, Amazon has a Kindle app that works on iPhone and iPad devices, which means you can read the same ebook on both your Kindle and other devices.

Multi-functional devices such as the Apple iPhone and iPod Touch are also an increasingly popular alternative to ebook readers. These Apple devices are smaller than the ebook readers, which means that the screen is smaller too, but they do fit into your pocket. The type of screen on the iPhone is also very different to that found on ebook readers. Where ebook readers offer a matt grey-on-grey display designed to be easy on the eye for prolonged reading, as well as using minimal battery power, the iPhone's display is glossy and bright, which makes it harder to use as an ebook reader for long periods of time.

One of the most popular alternatives to an ebook reader is the iPad. So if, as an avid reader, you're considering buying one rather than a dedicated ebook reader here are some advantages and disadvantages of the iPad for reading ebooks.

The advantages of using an Apple iPad as an ebook reader

▶ The iPad screen – at 9.7in (24.5cm) – is bigger than that of most ebook readers. Yet the device is still compact and lightweight, which makes it easy to carry and hold.

▶ The iPad is a multi-functional device – it can be used for surfing the internet, reading and sending email, enjoying photos, watching videos, listening to music, playing games, as well as reading ebooks.

▶ The iPad comes with access to iBooks, where iPad users can browse and purchase ebooks from more than 100,000 titles from major and independent publishers. Although there aren't as many ebooks available as on Amazon, you can – as with the Amazon Kindle DX – buy ebooks on the go.

The disadvantages of using an Apple iPad as an ebook reader

▶ The iPad features a high-resolution glossy colour screen – as found on most laptops. This makes reading less comfortly than on a device that has an electronic ink screen.

▶ The iPad's ten hours of battery life do not compare to the two or more weeks of use on standard ebook readers. If you plan to take your iPad on holiday with you, or use it when travelling, this could be a big issue.

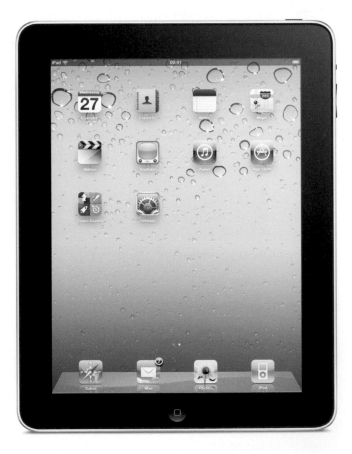

▶ Although you can import and read copyright-free ePub books on your iPad, iBooks can be read only on Apple devices

▶ With prices starting at £429, the iPad is more expensive than many ebook readers.

SMART PHONES

By reading and following all the steps in this chapter, you will get to grips with:

▶ **Essential smartphone features**

▶ **Choosing the right smartphone**

▶ **Setting up email and contacts**

▶ Smartphones

Jargon buster

PDA
PDA stands for Personal Digital Assistant. These are standalone mini-computers used primarily as electronic organisers with support for calendars, address books, email, notes and so on.

GSM
GSM – or Global System for Mobile Communications – is the standard mobile phone technology used in the UK. It is the second generation (2G) network standard that the overwhelming majority of voice calls and texts are transmitted over.

WiMax
WiMax (Worldwide Interoperability for Microwave Access) uses radio waves to provide wireless internet access to digital devices. Similar to Wi-Fi, WiMAX supports faster data transfer and a greater range of coverage with access up to 30 miles from a base station.

SMARTPHONES EXPLAINED

Once the preserve of business people, smartphones have become one of the must-have devices for anyone wanting to stay connected wherever they are.

Combining traditional mobile phone tools with powerful computing features, smartphones can perform a number of different functions, such as playing music, taking pictures, surfing the internet and running applications.

Smartphones are sometimes confused with 'feature phones', which are lower-priced handsets that can also access the internet and perform similar multimedia tasks.

The difference is that smartphones have much more powerful computer processors, and run a complete 'operating system', in the same way your home PC runs an operating system such as Windows. In many ways, smartphones are more like pocket PCs or PDAs (personal digital assistants) than mobile phones.

Along with the ability to make and receive mobile phone calls, a smartphone will also have some or all of the following:

▶ A more powerful and computer-like operating system
▶ A larger screen – usually a touchscreen
▶ A full qwerty keyboard (either on-screen, or a physical keyboard)
▶ The ability to run numerous applications and productivity software tools such as word processors, spreadsheets, organisers, email and web browsers
▶ Multimedia features that let you take and view pictures and video in many formats
▶ Multiple connectivity possibilities – not only standard GSM for making phone calls but also 3G, Wi-Fi and even WiMax connections to surf the internet. A smartphone can also easily connect to a local area network (LAN)
▶ The ability to easily transfer data to your computer and other devices through USB cables or Bluetooth adapters

Operating systems

Just like computers, smartphones have operating systems and there are several different types available.

Apple's iPhone uses an operating system based on the Mac OS X, while the Google-developed Android OS can be found on a number of smartphones including HTC's Desire and Samsung's Galaxy S. Microsoft launched a Windows Phone 7 at the end of 2010 to better compete with Apple and Android devices, while BlackBerry smartphones use the RIM operating system.

Nokia's Symbian operating system is used on its Nokia smartphones, as well as those from a few other manufacturers. Although Symbian smartphones have some good features, the operating system isn't as easy to use as Apple's iOS or Android Google.

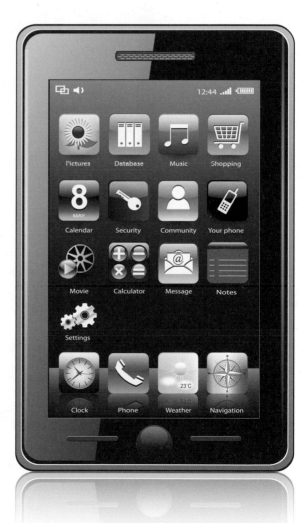

One of the early pioneers of the smartphone market, Palm has been making smartphones since 2002 and its operating system – the Palm OS – is older still, having been originally developed in 1996 for use on PDAs. Despite the popularity of products such as the Palm Pilot, it has lost ground to competitors such as Apple. Its webOS – a new easy-to-use operating system with good features – was unveiled in 2009, but it has been hampered by the lack of available apps when compared to the iPhone.

Palm was bought by HP in 2010 and its new products rebranded. In February 2011, HP announced two new webOS smartphones – the Pre 3 and the Veer – along the HP TouchPad – a rival to the iPad.

▶ Smartphones

SMARTPHONES TOUR

HIGH-SPEED INTERNET
You can browse web pages, access email, watch videos online, and download apps and music.

LARGER SCREEN
Smartphones have larger and better-quality screens than standard mobile phones.

ACCESS TO APPS
Most smartphones have a button that will instantly access the location where apps can be bought and downloaded directly to the handset.

EMAIL
Access to an email account is standard on most smartphones, although on some models this may be limited to web mail.

TOUCHSCREEN
Many smartphones offer touchscreens which allow you to navigate menus by tapping or dragging icons directly on the screen.

MAKE CALLS
Smartphones make calls just like a standard mobile phone, across your mobile provider's network.

MUSIC PLAYER
Most smartphones can play music files.

FULL QWERTY KEYPAD
Some smartphones come with a full qwerty keypad similar to a laptop or desktop keyboard, which makes typing emails and text messages easier.

▶ Smartphones

TIP

Which? Mobile features a round-up of the best camera phones.

SMARTPHONE FEATURES

Not all smartphones offer the same features, but the ones listed should be available on most devices.

High-speed internet access

A great deal of a smartphone's functionality relies on it being able to access the internet, allowing you to browse web pages, access email, watch online videos, and download apps and music.

Music player

Nearly all smartphones should be able to play music files in the same way as a dedicated MP3 player. Some also have a built-in FM radio. However, be warned that the sound quality can often be inferior to a dedicated device. If playing music is important, look for a mobile that allows you to plug in your own headphones, as the ones supplied may not be of great quality.

Camera

Most smartphones are able to take pictures and record video. If these are features you'll use often, make sure you check the camera quality, as it can vary quite considerably between different smartphones. Typical mobile camera resolutions are now at least 3Mp (megapixel, see page 76). This falls short of digital camera quality, but some phones have resolutions of 8Mp and proper flashes. Some smartphones – including the iPhone 4 – even let you take reasonable quality video.

Touchscreen

Smartphone touchscreens were popularised by Apple's iPhone, and have since been used by many other smartphone manufacturers.

There are two main types of smartphone touchscreens – resistive and capacitive.

Capacitive is the more advanced touchscreen technology and offers more accurate control (see page 73).

Touchscreens can be divisive when it comes to their usability. Some people find it awkward to type on a touchscreen keypad, while others would never think of going back to regular buttons, so it's a good idea to try out a touchscreen phone before you buy one.

Qwerty keyboard

Smartphones typically use a qwerty keyboard, similar to the one found on laptop keyboards, with the letters laid out in the standard manner. Compared to a traditional mobile phone, this is a faster way to enter text and compose lengthy emails than pecking around a numeric keypad and using predictive text entry.

Many smartphones, including the iPhone 4, have virtual keyboards on their touchscreens that let you tap an image of a letter to register a keystroke. BlackBerry smartphones still mainly use a physical keyboard, although the keys are very small.

Applications

Applications, or 'apps', are a key feature of smartphones. They broaden the functionality of your phone, in a similar way to the software you buy for your PC. See 'Smartphone Apps' on page 140.

Smartphones

SMARTPHONE BATTERIES

Smartphones are more powerful devices than mobile phones and require a lot of power to run. This inevitably places high demands on the phone's battery, and some smartphones are notorious for running out of battery power after barely a day's use.

So, knowing more about your battery, how it works, and how you can improve its efficiency, can be very useful.

Type of battery

Most modern mobile and smartphone batteries are Lithium-ion batteries. This form of battery is favoured in consumer electronic devices, particularly portable ones, due to its energy-to-weight ratio.

They're particularly good for mobile phones as they have no memory effect, meaning that they don't lose large amounts of their maximum charge capacity, like some nickel cadmium batteries.

Replacing a battery

For most phones, replacing a battery is a reasonably straightforward affair.

First, turn off your phone. Usually, you can take out the battery by removing the back of your phone and prising it out with your fingers. As a rule of thumb, if you can't remove the casing with pressure applied by your hands, then it's not supposed to move.

Most phone backs are either slide or clip mounted. Make sure you know which one your phone is before you try to open it. Slide backs will require firm but gentle pressure applied through the parallel axis of your phone, while clip fixings can usually be pulled away from the body with a strong fingernail.

Once you have your phone open, the battery usually sits on top of the Sim card and can simply be pulled out.

There should be three small golden plates on one edge of the battery, to match three connectors in the phone. If you make sure these are lined up when you insert the new battery, you shouldn't have any problems.

With some phones – most notably the Apple iPhone – you cannot replace the batteries yourself. Instead, you will have to send the phone back to the manufacturer.

Tips to maximise battery life

There are a number of general measures you can apply to increase your smartphone's battery life. Most smartphones allow you turn off functions that drain battery power, and these can normally be accessed in the phone's Settings menu, but if in doubt check your manual. Remember, you can quickly turn on the functions again when you need them.

▶ As heat degrades battery life, don't leave your smartphone lying about in the direct sunlight or in the car on a hot day
▶ Dim the backlight of your screen – a simple function that nearly every smartphone has. Slightly reducing the brightness of the screen won't make much difference to the display, but can make a noticeable difference to the life of the battery
▶ Use a plain, black background wallpaper
▶ Even if you're not using the internet directly, smartphones will periodically check online for email messages, instant messages and data updates, then alert you immediately. To save battery life, turn off push notification (see page 156) in your phone's Settings. Also increase the interval between when the smartphone checks for new email messages or, better still, set it to check for messages manually
▶ Temporarily disable any Wi-Fi or mobile internet connections, when you're not using them
▶ If you rarely use a Bluetooth headset or car kit, consider turning off Bluetooth
▶ GPS can drain battery life, so turn this off unless you really need it
▶ Turn off vibrate when playing games on your smartphone
▶ Make sure apps are turned off when you're not using them. In some smartphones, if an app is not exited fully it keeps working in the background
▶ Use an app to monitor and reduce your power output

Other battery options

There are plenty of ideas out there for dealing with battery life problems. Cases that have a built-in battery are useful, as are temporary (and very small) power boosters that can be kept in wallets to offer an extra jolt of power in an emergency.

Third-party extended life batteries are also an option. They don't add any weight or size to your current battery, but are simply higher quality. This means they can extend the life of a single charge quite significantly.

▶ Smartphones

APPLE IPHONE EXPLAINED

Apple iPhones are one of the most popular lines of smartphones on the market.

As with many other smartphones, iPhones can perform a number of functions. As well as the basic tasks you would expect of a mobile phone, such as texts and voice calls, iPhones are also capable of taking pictures, playing music, surfing the internet and running a large number of different applications.

Apple has released four different iPhone models to date:

▶ iPhone
▶ iPhone 3G
▶ iPhone 3GS
▶ iPhone 4

Each iPhone iteration made some improvements on its predecessor.

The iPhone 3G enabled users to connect to 3G mobile internet networks, moderately improved the iPhone's battery life, and added GPS support, while the iPhone 3GS improved the processor speed, battery life and camera quality.

The latest model, the iPhone 4, improved the iPhone's display, processor and added an extra camera to the front of the handset for video calls.

The iPhone and iPhone 3G are both discontinued, and it's likely that the iPhone 3GS will see the same fate soon to make way for newer models.

Advantages of an iPhone

One of the most useful functions of any iPhone is its ability to access the internet. As long as you have access to a mobile or Wi-Fi network, you can connect to the internet and browse web pages.

▶ This connectivity also allows you to check and reply to emails, as well as download many different applications, from bus timetables to video games.

▶ All iPhone models feature capacitive touchscreens (see page 74), which generally make browsing web pages a more comfortable experience.

▶ Though, when it comes to more basic tasks such as texting and accessing menus, opinions are often divided regarding the benefits of a touchscreen over a regular keypad.

▶ The latest iPhone, the iPhone 4, features video calling, or FaceTime as Apple calls it. This allows you to see the person you're calling, and vice versa, while you speak to them. All iPhone models also let you take photographs and play music.

Disadvantages of an iPhone

▶ Adobe Flash software is not supported by the iPhone's web browser, meaning some web pages do not display correctly

▶ Older models do not support multi-tasking (running numerous applications at the same time)

▶ The iPhone 4's voice call signal strength allegedly suffers if you grip the phone in a certain way

USING THE APPLE IPHONE APP STORE

The Apple iPhone App Store allows you to download applications, either paid-for or free, for use on your iPhone or iPod Touch.

To use, simply enter the App Store via the App Store icon on your iPhone, and use the search tool to identify what kind of app you want. The apps are categorized, so finding the right one isn't too hard.

Once you've selected your app, the payment process is simple. Just follow the on-screen prompts and your app will be installed and running in moments.

You can either download apps from the App Store straight to your handset, or you can download them to your Mac or PC through iTunes. Once the apps are on your computer, you can transfer them to your phone. Downloading to your PC or Mac means you have a backup of the app should you accidently delete it from your iPhone.

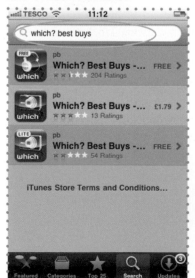

Finding the right apps

The app store separates applications in a number of ways. You can search by name, topic, or just browse through the entire catalogue.

The apps are categorised, so for instance a tip calculator app will be in the food and drink section, while an expenses manager will be with the business apps.

Each app is given a rating and review on the app store, so you can find out exactly what other people think of that app, and how well it works.

iPhone App Store versus Android Market

The number of free applications on the App Store is somewhat limited compared to the Android Market (see page 152). Around 30 per cent of apps are free on Apple's store, compared with over 50 per cent for the Android Market.

Apple exercises tight control over which apps are allowed on the iPhone, which makes the iPhone App Store more secure than Android's Market. This does make the range of apps slightly less diverse.

One area where the App Store has an advantage over Android's Market is video games. Some of the biggest videogame developers have been making games for the iPhone, and the quality of iPhone games is generally better than Android games. This is largely because Android runs on so many different handsets, with different capabilities, making it harder for developers to optimise their games. So if you're heavily into gaming then, currently, the iPhone is the best choice of handset.

iPhone App Store versus BlackBerry App World

While BlackBerry's App World store pales in comparison to the sheer volume of different apps found on the iPhone App Store, it does offer some unique features yet to make the jump to the iPhone. While the iPhone App Store charges your iTunes account for downloads, App World uses a range of payments, including PayPal and direct billing to your mobile phone account. Although lots of apps on App World are US-centric, it is well-served with business applications.

DOWNLOAD AN APP FROM THE ITUNES STORE

There are thousands of apps to choose from on the iTunes store. See page 101 for how to download iTunes and set up an account.

1 Connect your iPhone to your computer using either your FireWire or USB cables

2 Open iTunes

3 On the left hand side of the screen, click on **iTunes Store**

4 There are multiple options available for choosing, selecting and buying apps. Click the **Apps** label located in the centre of the screen, then from the list that appears browse to find something you like.

To refine your search, scroll down the screen and choose either **Top Free Apps** or **Top Paid Apps** on the right of the screen. This will show you the top 100 free or paid-for apps you can download or buy.

To search for an app, enter its name or a keyword into the search box on the top-right of the screen

5 To find out more about an app, click on its icon or name. This will show the app page, which has information about the app. You can view screens of the app, ensure it compatible with your model of iPhone, and read customer reviews

6 If you want to buy the app, click the **Buy app** button. At the prompt, type in your iTunes account login name and password. Once entered, the app will download to your copy of iTunes on your computer

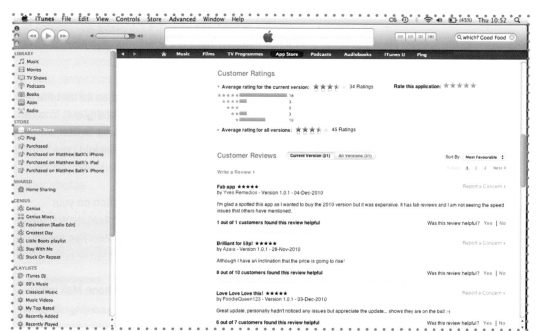

7 Make sure that you have your iPhone set to install all apps. To do this, click on your iPhone on the left-hand panel of the iTunes screen.

The main panel will now show information about your iPhone. Click the **apps** tab at the top of the screen. Here you can select which apps you wish to sync to your iPhone, as well as arrange how they will appear on your iPhone's screens. Enjoy using your new app.

TRY THIS

iTunes will automatically notify you when a new version is available. If so, when you launch iTunes, a dialog box will pop up asking if you want to download and install this new version. Click **Download iTunes** and follow the prompts to install the new software.

▶ Smartphones

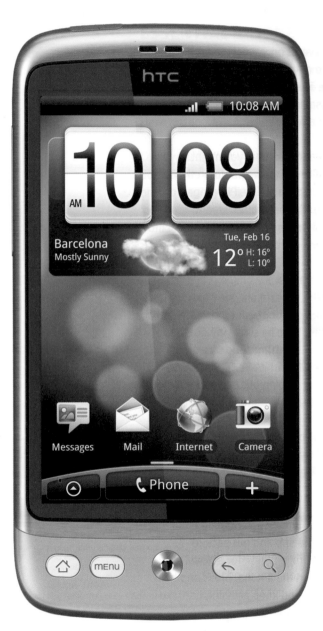

ANDROID SMARTPHONES EXPLAINED

The result of a partnership between Google and Android Inc, the Android brand is becoming increasingly visible on the mobile phone market. But rather than being a mobile phone operator, or a handset manufacturer, Android is an operating system (OS) that can be found on a range of smartphones.

A smartphone OS is basically the platform from which you use all your phone's functions. It works in the same way as the operating system on a home PC, such as Windows.

One of the reasons Android is proving so popular with phone manufacturers is its 'open source' software. This essentially means that anyone can help to develop the software, without paying licence fees. This is unlike a 'closed source' OS such as Windows, which is developed only by Microsoft and its associates.

Also, unlike most closed source operating systems, Android is free to use, so manufacturers, such as Samsung and HTC, don't have to pay anyone to include it on their phones, and they don't have to spend money developing their own OS.

Advantages of Android smartphones

▶ The most important benefit of an open source operating system (OS) such as Android is that you'll get a wider range of developer expertise going into your phone's OS and its updates, which should result in a much more stable and efficient platform

▶ Generally, Android smartphone applications are cheaper when compared with other operating systems

▶ Android smartphones are proving popular and, given that the OS is also supported by Google, Android will probably be around for quite some time. This means that your phone's OS will be frequently updated and developers will continue to make apps for it

Disadvantages of Android smartphones

▶ As Android is open source, many phone manufacturer have tinkered with the operating system, to add new features, or make it easier to use. However, this means that not all Android apps are compatible with every Android device

▶ Unlike Apple's iPhone, different Android phones can sometimes offer quite diverse user interfaces (UI). Sometimes this works well (HTC has been particularly successful in modifying Android), but sometimes it doesn't. These different interfaces can also delay OS updates, as different manufacturers have to optimise each update to work with their own UI

▶ The other drawback is that because Android is built around open source principles, its apps store isn't tightly regulated in the same way as those run by Apple or Nokia. This can be a good thing, giving developers more creative freedom, but it also means that the likelihood of malicious apps finding their way on to the store is increased

Smartphones

USING THE ANDROID MARKET

The Android Market allows you to browse, buy and download a wide range of application software for your Android-based smartphone.

Accessing the Android Market is simple. Just find the Market icon on your smartphone – it is usually in the same menu as the rest of your apps. If you click this icon, you'll be taken directly to the store.

Remember, your smartphone needs to be connected to the internet to access the Android Market. (See page 180 for how to connect your phone to the internet.)

The store is divided into apps, games and downloads.

'Apps' will show you general applications, divided into further categories such as news, health and work, whereas 'Games' will show you the variety of video games available for download.

The 'downloads' category will show you the apps you have already downloaded and if there are any updates for them. You can also separate the various sections by 'Paid' and 'Free', allowing you to search for either free or paid apps.

Android Market doesn't let you download apps to anywhere other than your phone. You can browse new additions, away from your phone, on the official website, but to download anything, you need to access the mobile site.

Finding the right apps

One of the great things about Android Market is that so much of its content is free to download, and a majority of the paid apps have a free version (often subsidised by advertising), sometimes called a 'lite' version.

Thousands of apps are added every month, so finding the right one could be tricky. The best way to find what you're looking for is to use the search tool located in the upper right-hand corner.

TRY THIS

Another great feature of the Android Market is the reviews section. It's always advisable to read app reviews as some may not work very well, or may even break your phone.

For instance, if you want a hotel booking app, simply type in 'hotel', or 'hotel booking', just as you would in a standard search bar, and you will see all the apps related to that search term.

▶ Smartphones

Jargon buster

Widget
A graphic element and program that lets the user interact with an application or the OS. It can be used to perform a simple function, such as accessing a calculator or calendar, with only one click or keystroke.

ESSENTIAL ANDROID TIPS
Google's Android is one of the most popular smartphone operating systems, appearing on a wide range of handsets designed by some of the biggest mobile phone manufacturers, such as HTC, Samsung and LG.

To get the most out of your Android smartphone, check out the tips below.

Change your ringtone for specific contacts
On the individual contacts page, for each entry in your phonebook, you will find a 'set ringtone' option. Here you can change the ringtone for when that person calls you.

Open multiple browser windows
When you're browsing the internet, just long press on any link, and you'll be given the option to open it in a new window. This can really help when cross-referencing information.

Return your apps
The Android Market will refund apps that you return within 15 minutes of buying them, in case you accidently purchase an app. Just visit the **My Downloads** page from the Market and select **Uninstall** and **Refund** on the relevant app.

Set up one-touch dialling
If you have someone you phone a lot, it's easy to set up a dialling widget on your phone's home screen to call that person with one touch. Just pick an empty space on your screen and long press to bring up a menu. Select **Shortcuts**, then **Contacts**, and select a contact from the list.

Start again
If you ever need to clear your phone or reset it, simply activate a hard reset. In the **Security** menu, in **Settings**, you'll find **Factory data reset**.

Customise your language
You can add or delete words from your Android smartphone dictionary.

1 Go to **Settings**, then **Language and Keyboard**, then **Touch Input**

2 Select the **User Dictionary** option.

3 Use the **Add Word** or the **Delete** function to customise your dictionary.

Customise your notification bar

You can add any apps you like to the bar at the top of the screen that scrolls down to reveal notifications. Just go to the **Market Place** and download **Bar Control**.

Manage your files

Using a file-managing app such as Astro will allow you to move your files around, as well as create and manage folders, just like you do on your home computer. (To find Astro just input its name into the search tool on the Android Market.) File managers can also 'kill' any unwanted apps running in the background, freeing up processing power.

Auto screen your calls

If you want a little peace and quiet from those people who are always pestering you, try sending their phone calls straight to voicemail. Just view their contact page and toggle the handy Send to Voicemail option to **On**.

Push email

This refers to how a mail server handles an email. In this case, as soon as your mail server receives an email, it 'pushes' it to your device. You are instantly notified that you have new mail and can read it immediately. Email on your laptop or other smartphones works on a 'pull' system called POP, which sees the device contact a mail server at regular intervals to download email.' This means there is a slight delay in receiving email.

RSS

RSS (Really Simple Syndication) is a way of sharing information about a website's new content, such as news headlines, with other websites or RSS readers. By subscribing to the RSS feed on your favourite website, you will be automatically alerted to new content via your web browser's RSS feed reader when it is available.

BLACKBERRY EXPLAINED

BlackBerry is a range of smartphones from Canadian company Research In Motion (RIM). Originally launched as a combination of PDA (personal data assistant) and mobile phone, BlackBerry is primarily known for its ability to send and receive (push) internet email wherever mobile network service coverage is present, or through Wi-Fi connectivity.

Over the last few years, BlackBerrys have been upgraded from only supporting email, text and phone calls, to having digital cameras, expandable memory, media players, internet access, Wi-Fi, GPS and pretty much every other feature you find on a smartphone.

However, the strength of a BlackBerry is still email, and it can handle email attachments such as Microsoft Word, Excel, PowerPoint documents, PDFs and images. Its reliability and easy integration with most companies' email systems means it's popular as a business tool.

RIM/BlackBerry OS 6

BlackBerry devices use a mobile operating system developed by RIM. The launch of the BlackBerry Torch in August 2010 saw the first use of the latest version of the operating system – BlackBerry 6.

BlackBerry 6 features a redesigned interface that works with a touchscreen and trackpad. Event notifications, such as new text messages or emails, can now be previewed on the redesigned homescreen without having to click through to apps. You can see your social and RSS feeds in one place and type an update once and send it to one, all or selected networks.

BlackBerry 6 has a new web browser that features tabs for accessing multiple sites simultaneously, an auto-wrap text zoom feature that can intelligently wrap text in a column while maintaining the placement of a page's key elements, and a pinch-to-zoom feature.

The media player in the new OS has been revamped. Now, similar to Apple's iTunes, it displays your music album artwork on a virtual carousel. From here you can flick through your albums, navigate through the track you're listening to, shuffle and repeat.

A powerful search tool has been added to the home screen. By clicking or tapping the Universal Search icon, you can search for any contact, content, app on the phone itself, the web or in the BlackBerry App World.

The new OS improves the way a BlackBerry handles photos, including a two-finger tap-to-edit feature, and a geo-location title for each picture to show the name of the city where it was taken. The picture files – which are named automatically – can then be found easily using Universal Search.

Apps that run on previous versions of the BlackBerry operating system will also run on OS 6.

BlackBerry App World

BlackBerry App World is pre-loaded on the BlackBerry Torch – a good addition as previously you had to download the app store to your phone.

The App World has also been updated. It now offers more than 5,000 apps, although this falls far short of the hundreds of thousands available on Apple's iPhone Apps store and Google's Android Market.

You can purchase apps and pay for them via your mobile phone bills.

▶ Smartphones

MICROSOFT WINDOWS PHONE 7

As with Google's Android OS, Microsoft's mobile operating system is available on a wide range of smartphones from manufacturers such as Dell, HTC Corp, LG and Samsung, as well as mobile operators including Vodafone, O2 and Orange.

The latest version of Microsoft's mobile OS, Windows 7 was launched in October 2010. The system was designed from scratch and the result is a mobile OS that looks like nothing else in the smartphone market.

The new Windows Phone 7 features a large, coloured tile layout that you can scroll vertically. Each tile provides access to a function – or 'hubs of information' as Microsoft calls them – such as phone, email, photos, people (contacts), games and so forth.

You can move the tiles around, delete them, or reorder them. A vertical menu on the right lists all of your apps and they can be added to and moved around the screen using a swipe of a finger.

The new minimum hardware specifications for the Windows Mobile 7 handsets, including a capacitive touchscreen, mean that the devices are faster and easier to use, and don't require a stylus.

As well as being a big leap forward in design, Windows Phone 7 is also packed with new features such as the Sound Enhancer, Microsoft Office – which features full support for Word, Excel and PowerPoint – a Photo Enhancer, Bing Search and Bing Maps. It also comes with cloud-based storage which means you can back up and save your files to a remote server via the internet.

Now that Xbox Live is integrated into Windows Phone 7, the new handsets allow you to play games online against other people.

Windows Phone 7's two multimedia tiles or hubs – Music + Video, and Pictures – are similar in appearance and functionality to Microsoft's portable music player the Zune HD.

Music + Video plays music, videos, and podcasts, and allows users to access the Zune Marketplace to buy music or rent it with the Zune Pass subscription service, as well as view artist biographies and photos.

The Pictures tile displays your Facebook and Windows Live photo albums, alongside photos taken with the phone's camera.

Jargon buster

Cloud computing
Cloud computing allows files and programs to be stored remotely on connected internet servers rather than locally on your computer hard drive. You can access your files from any device making it easy to share files with others who are authorised to access the same, shared storage space.

Smartphones

CHOOSING THE RIGHT ONE FOR YOU

Before buying an expensive smartphone, think carefully about whether or not you'll use its extra features.

If you're certain that you just want a phone for voice calls and texting, then it really isn't worth paying so much extra for a smartphone. There are many good quality budget phones you can buy for a fraction of the price.

But, if you're unfamiliar with smartphones, it can be hard to know how useful their features can be. This is because smartphones rely, to an extent, on users downloading individual apps to expand the functions of the phone.

The smartphone market has grown rapidly in recent years, and mobile phone manufacturers seem to be announcing new devices, with new features and capabilities, every month.

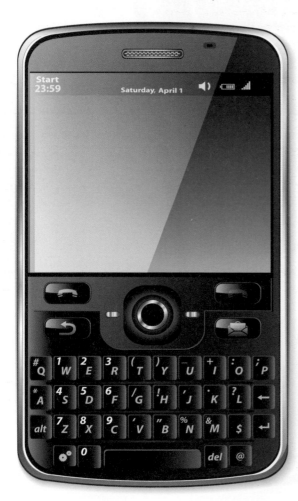

When comparing different smartphones you need to think carefully about what features you will use the most. It's no good buying a business-focused BlackBerry Curve, if you want to play games and enjoy multimedia applications.

Which smartphone operating system is the best?

There's no easy answer to this question. The smartphone market is extemely competitive with several rival software platforms: Android, iOS for iPhone, Symbian and all its variations, BlackBerry OS, webOS for Palm phones, and Windows Phone 7.

Each operating system has different strengths and weaknesses. Apple's iPhone iOS, for example, is slick, smart and simple enough for anyone to use, while Android is more open, with some innovative features such as turn-by-turn navigation and voice commands. RIM/BlackBerry OS is great for email, although, to date, its web browser has been poor.

Be careful not to get caught out buying a smartphone with an operating system that will receive few updates from the manufacturer. For example, now that Microsoft has released Windows Phone 7, it's unlikely it will offer many updates for previous Windows Mobile operating systems.

Extending functionality with apps

Many people choose a smartphone operating system based on the number and type of apps that can be downloaded and used. Different operating systems have access to different app stores, and while some apps are available across different stores, others are not.

At the moment, the iPhone is considered the best when it comes to the quality and breadth of applications, although Android is fast catching up.

However, the best smartphone for you isn't necessarily the one with the most apps available to install. Consider how you will use a smartphone to work out what are essential features.

Design

Size and weight, along with screen size and resolution, make a difference in the display and handling of smartphones, so if possible try before you buy.

Music and photos

Compare the quality of each handset's camera (the higher the resolution the better) and compare the type of flash it uses as, typically, a Xenon generally results in better pictures than an LED flash.

With music-playing phones you obviously need to consider the sound quality, but also think about how you store your music. For instance, if you use Apple's popular iTunes to manage and download tracks, then an iPhone is a good choice to ensure compatibility.

If your music is stored in a format other than MP3, then pay attention to which file formats are supported by the handset.

Connectivity

A key aspect of a smartphone's functionality relies on the internet, such as browsing web pages, streaming video and downloading apps. So, when comparing smartphones, pay attention to how they access the internet.

Wi-Fi is usually standard on smartphones and you should avoid buying a handset that doesn't support it.

A mobile internet connection takes place over your mobile provider's network. There are different types of connections that offer different speeds. The most common are GPRS, EDGE, 3G and HSDPA.

HSDPA currently offers the quickest connection speed, so if you plan on using mobile internet a lot, then make sure your phone will support this type of connection.

Ports

As you're likely to store music on your smartphone, make sure the model you buy has a 3.5mm (0.9in) audio socket so you can use your own headphones. A micro USB port is also useful as, increasingly, it's becoming the standard for connecting and charging phones.

Most smartphones have plenty of internal storage, but if you are a heavy user of music and video, look for a smartphone with a MicroSD slot as this will let you add up to 32GB of external storage.

Touchscreen or keypad

The Apple iPhone introduced most of the world to touchscreen smartphones in 2007, and ever since then touchscreen technology has been employed in hundreds of devices.

Touchscreens offer intuitive controls – such as pinching the screen to zoom-in – and the capacity for a much larger display, in order to better enjoy pictures and video.

But not all users enjoy using touchscreens. Some prefer full qwerty keypads, such as those featured on most BlackBerry phones.

If you're unsure about whether you want a touchscreen device or a regular keypad, try a touchscreen for yourself.

However, be aware that, as with any new technology, touchscreens can take some getting used to. So while you may find using a touchscreen awkward at first, you might change your mind after a few days.

There are a few smartphone models, such as the Motorola Milestone, that offer both touchscreen and keypad.

Costs and contracts

Of course, one of the key factors when choosing a smartphone will be the costs involved. There's no denying that the best new smartphone models are expensive, especially as you may have to pay for the model upfront, as well as a monthly fee, for several years. However, if you're prepared to compromise on various features, such as a smaller or lower resolution screen, you can save yourself a great deal. (See page 164.)

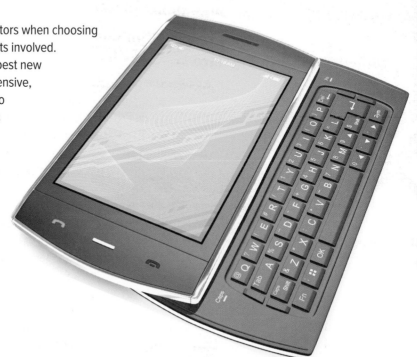

▶ Smartphones

BUYING A SMARTPHONE

The best way to pick through the many deals and payment plans is to use a comparision website such as Which? Mobile's online comparison tool (www.which.co.uk/mobile/). Not only can you compare different smartphone models, you can see what's involved on the payment front too.

There are three main ways of paying for your smartphone and its use: pay-as-you-go (PAYG), pay monthly contract and SIM-only contract

The best option depends on how you use your smartphone for calls and web-surfing, and how often you want to upgrade to a new handset.

Pay-as-you-go (PAYG) mobile tariffs

With a PAYG tariff there's no fixed monthly fee. Instead, you pay by 'topping up' your smartphone credit in advance. You can get top-up vouchers in many high street stores, or you can top-up online, by phone or text. Once you've used up all your credit, you won't be able to make outgoing calls or texts until you top up again.

PAYG advantages

- ▶ You only pay for the call minutes/texts you use
- ▶ You can only use your phone when there's credit on it, limiting the risk of running up unexpectedly high bills
- ▶ It's suited to light users and those under 18, as you don't have to sign up to a mobile contract
- ▶ No credit check
- ▶ You can end your PAYG deal whenever you want to without a penalty

PAYG disadvantages

- ▶ You'll probably have to pay full price for a handset up-front
- ▶ Fewer mobile models to choose from
- ▶ Some operators require a minimum PAYG mobile top-up to qualify for certain incentives (such as free weekend calls)
- ▶ Calls per minute and texts may cost more than when paying monthly
- ▶ You must top up every time your credit runs out

Pay monthly mobile contracts

With a traditional mobile contract, you pay a fixed minimum monthly fee by direct debit and get a free or subsidised smartphone as well as a fixed number of inclusive call minutes and texts. You'll have to commit to a 12-, 18- or 24-month contract.

WATCH OUT!

Check the terms and conditions that fix your mobile handset to a particular mobile network – you pay a fee to 'unlock' it in order to sign up with another provider when the contract ends.

Pay monthly advantages
- There's a greater choice of smartphone handsets
- The latest smartphones may be available
- If you stay within your usage cap, you'll never pay more than your minimum monthly fee
- You'll never be left without a mobile phone service because your credit has run out

Pay monthly disadvantages
- You must agree to a minimum 12-, 18- or 24-month contract.
- If you cancel early you may be charged a lump sum to cover all of the monthly payments for the remainder of your contract
- Your minimum payment is fixed, whether or not you use all your mobile call minutes/texts
- If you exceed your usage cap, you'll have to pay extra for each additional minute or text
- Calls to some numbers, such as international calls or calls to 0800 or 0870 numbers, won't be part of your inclusive minutes and will be billed on top of your minimum monthly fee
- If you have a poor credit rating, you may have problems getting accepted for a contract

WATCH OUT!
If you don't use your PAYG phone for a long period, your provider may assume it's no longer in use and deactivate the number. You may then lose any credit that's on the phone. To avoid this, use your phone at least once every three months so that the provider knows it is active.

SIM-only contracts
With a SIM-only deal you get a new mobile SIM card but not a handset. SIM-only contracts usually tie you in for only 30 days at a time.

SIM-only advantages
- More flexible than lengthy mobile contracts
- You'll get more mobile minutes/texts for your money than with a mobile contract that includes a handset
- You can save up to £15 a month compared with traditional pay monthly mobile tariffs with equivalent minutes and texts

SIM-only disadvantages
- No free or subsidised mobile phone
- You might have to unlock an existing smartphone with a new mobile service provider
- If you want a top-of-the-range handset, you might be better off with a traditional contract

▶ Smartphones

SETTING UP A SMARTPHONE

A smartphone is much like any other mobile phone to set up. At its most basic, you insert a SIM card to enable it to connect to the mobile phone operator's network, then you can make calls, store numbers and start accessing email.

The set-up for different brands of mobile phone is slightly different, but most follow a similar principle to setting up an iPhone, which is used in the following example.

1 Apple's iPhone requires iTunes to be downloaded and installed on a Mac or Windows PC. Download it from www.apple.com/uk/itunes. Follow the download and installation instructions on page 101 for setting up an iTunes account

2 Modern smartphones use a special SIM card called a MicroSIM. Using the SIM eject tool that comes with the iPhone, open the MicroSIM tray found on the side of the iPhone, insert the card, and slide it back into the iPhone. Other smartphones may have the SIM tray located beneath the battery

3 Press the power button to turn on the iPhone. The iPhone will display an image on the screen of a USB cable and the iTunes logo. Connect the cable to the iPhone, and the other end to the Mac or Windows PC or laptop that you downloaded iTunes on to in Step 1

4 Follow the on-screen instructions to activate your iPhone. The phone will also perform a basic sync with your laptop or desktop PC. From now on, any music, videos or apps you download on the PC will be transferred to the iPhone the next time you connect it using USB

Setting up email and calendars on a smartphone

Most smartphones use webmail services – such as Google Gmail, Yahoo! Ymail, and Windows Live – that will sync your email, calendar and contacts information across your PC, smartphone and on the web. Smartphones can also use Microsoft Exchange to connect to work email services – your IT department will be able to help set up access to Microsoft Exchange if you need this.

To connect to a free webmail service such as Google Gmail, do the following. If you already have a webmail account, then skip to Step 4.

1 Using a laptop or desktop PC, start your web browser and type www.gmail.com into the address bar of the web browser, then press Enter and wait for the page to load

2 Click the **Create an account** button on the right-hand side of the web browser screen. Fill in the details, choosing a Login Name. This will form the first part of your gmail.com email address. Enter a password and security question and make sure you note down the Login Name and email address (which is your LoginName@gmail.com), password and security question and answer. Fill in the remaining sections, then click **I accept. Create my account** button

3 Gmail will ask to text you a verification code to help prevent spam. Enter your mobile phone number, and click **Verify**. You'll get a text message – enter the code from the text message into the verification code box, and click **Verify**. On the following screen, click **Show me my account**. You'll be presented with your inbox, plus access to calendar services. Next, you need to get access to these on your smartphone

4 Switch on your iPhone, and on the Home Screen, press **Settings**, then scroll down and press **Mail, Contacts, Calendars**

5 On the following screen, press **Add Account**, then press **Gmail**

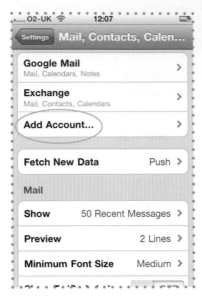

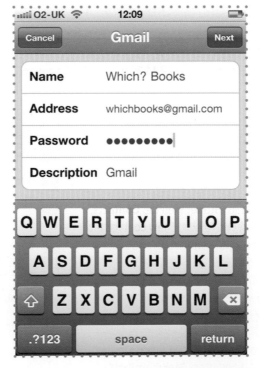

6 Enter your name, the Gmail address (LoginName@gmail. com), the password, and give the account a name, such as My Gmail Account. Click **Next** when done, and the account will verify

7 Choose which services – such as Mail, Calendars and Notes – to sync, then press **Save**. Once done, press the **Home** button to return to the Home Screen

8 Press **Mail**, and you'll see your inbox, sent mail and various folders from the webmail account you created earlier. Click on **Inbox** to read email

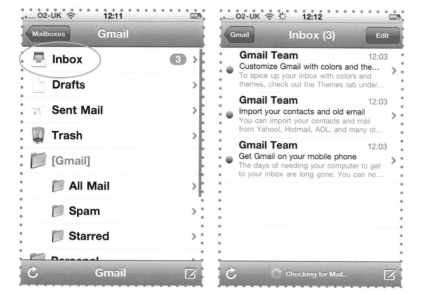

9 To create an email, press the pencil icon on the lower right of the screen. Enter the email address, subject and type the email message. Once done, press **Send**

Adding contacts to a smartphone

All smartphones allow you to easily add phone numbers and contact details of family and friends. Here's how to do it, using the iPhone as an example.

1 Turn on the iPhone, then tap **Phone**, then tap **Contacts**. This displays a list of contacts. To add a new contact, tap the + button in the upper-right corner

2 Enter the information in each of the fields, such as name, company, email address and phone numbers. To add a photo, click the **Add photo** button, and you can either take a photo on the spot using the camera, or pick one from the library on your iPhone. Tap **Save** when done. Whenever this contact calls, you'll now see their photo so you know who is calling

Smartphones

SMARTPHONE SECURITY

The issue of smartphone security has been growing over the last few years. Because of the rapid growth of the smartphone market, many new users have not been made aware of the potential risks these devices pose.

Most of us are now careful to dispose of any paperwork that can give away personal information to fraudsters, but a smartphone probably contains just as much sensitive data as anything you keep in a file at home.

Smartphones can be used to access your email accounts, and any information inside them, your social networks, what you search for on the internet, as well as the websites you visit.

If you use popular travel applications such as Google Maps, or Ovi Maps, fraudsters can even see which locations you've visited and, perhaps, figure out where you live.

This vast amount of personal information can be retrieved either by malware (malicious software), or by the theft of your handset.

Another growing risk to smartphones is 'silent activation'. This is where malware is installed on your phone and makes calls to premium telephone numbers set up by a hacker. These calls can rack up huge bills without your knowledge.

Each type of smartphone operating system has its own separate risks. The iPhone, for example, has a 'sandbox' configuration, which stops applications communicating with the phone, theoretically making the OS more secure. But recent advances in multi-tasking technology mean the iPhone may be more at risk than previously thought.

Android phones are more closely related to PC operating system structures and, therefore, potentially provide a relatively easy target for hackers.

One of the biggest problems for the Android operating system is that its apps market is built on an open model, with few quality controls, making it easier for malicious apps to find their way on to your phone.

The Windows, BlackBerry and Symbian systems are also at risk. It's not always malicious intent that opens your phone to abuse. Sloppy programming can leave 'doorways' into your phone for hackers to find. Similarly, it's possible for reputable app creators to have their distributor code stolen and malicious apps published under their name.

Keeping your smartphone safe

Smartphones, like all mobile phones, are natural targets for thieves and – given how much we now rely on them and the type of information we store on them – a lost handset can cost you more than just money. See page 205 for advice on how to protect your smartphone from theft.

As with any mobile device that connects to the Internet, smartphones are at risk from malware and information theft. Here are some to top tips to avoid this.

Download apps from recognised sites

Downloaded apps are the easiest route into your phone for hackers. By only buying from the dedicated app stores, and not 'jailbreaking', or opening up your phone for non-regulated software, you're already taking the first step towards keeping your phone safe.

A sizeable majority of malware found on phones currently comes from pirated software, due to hackers taking a popular app, adding their own malicious code and distributing it for free. So make sure you look for the official versions.

Block premium calls and texts from your smartphone

Minimise the charges that criminals can rack up. Mobile operators allow you to put a block on calling premium rate 09 numbers or texting premium rate short codes such as (88888). So, if you don't call premium 09 numbers, or use premium text numbers such as those used for voting in reality TV shows, get them blocked by your mobile provider.

Keep your mobile phone updated

Update your smartphone's operating system as often as you can, as these usually update the built-in security of your phone. Even if you have a brand new phone, check with your operator to see if there is a system update. The user's manual will explain how to be notified of, and download, updates.

Restrict Bluetooth and Wi-Fi usage

Turn off your Wi-Fi and Bluetooth functionality when you're not using them, as these are two possible routes into your phone. Check with the manual to find out how to do this.

Anti-virus protection

There are some mobile anti-virus packages out there. PhoneGuard Mobile Security is one specially designed for mobile devices, and covers most of the major operating systems. Given the relative youth of smartphone hacking, there's little evidence as yet to say if these security programs work well enough to warrant the purchase price. But, if you're the cautious type, they can be found for around £30.

In addition, there are a number of phone loss apps that will delete any sensitive information you have on your phone if it is lost or stolen, minimising the risk of data theft.

GETTING ONLINE

By reading and following all the steps in this chapter, you will get to grips with:

Mobile broadband and Wi-Fi

Syncing mobile devices

Streaming media to other devices

GOING ONLINE WITH MOBILE BROADBAND

The main advantage of owning a laptop, netbook or mobile device is the freedom to use it anywhere. While you can connect your laptop to the internet via your home router using a cable, this defeats one of the advantages of having a laptop.

If you want to send emails, surf the web, watch streaming video clips, and download files – while still enjoying the freedom to move around – it's best to connect to the internet wirelessly.

There are two ways your mobile device can connect to the internet wirelessly: Wi-Fi and 3G (known as mobile internet or broadband).

Some mobile devices, such as laptops, are capable of both technologies. But, while some ISPs (Internet Service Providers) provide both 3G and Wi-Fi internet connectivity, they typically treat them as individual services that require separate subscriptions and payments. So it helps to understand what each technology offers.

Mobile broadband (3G)

3G or mobile broadband uses the mobile phone network to allow you to access the internet on your mobile device almost anywhere – even when you're abroad. As with traditional fixed-line broadband, you can send emails, surf the web, watch streaming video clips and download files – all without being tied to a single location.

Some mobile devices, such as smartphones and certain types of tablet PCs, may have 3G capabilities built-in. With most laptops you will need a small USB modem – often called a dongle – to give you access to the internet wherever there's a 3G mobile signal (see page 180 for more on laptops and mobile broadband).

Buying mobile broadband

There are two main types of mobile broadband tariff – pay as you go (PAYG) and monthly contract. Most mobile broadband providers offer both.

Pay as you go (PAYG) mobile broadband

PAYG mobile broadband packages don't work in quite the same way as PAYG mobile phone tariffs.

You usually have to pay up-front for credit that gives you a specific amount of mobile broadband time (any period from a day to a month, depending on the provider) rather than paying per megabyte (MB) of data you actually use – although there will usually be a cap on your total data use.

The big advantage of PAYG is that you can cancel at any point without a penalty charge, so it's easy to change your mind or switch to another provider. This makes PAYG the best bet if you're not sure if mobile broadband will suit your needs, or you want to test network coverage before committing to a contract.

The downside is that you'll have to pay for your mobile broadband laptop dongle up front, and monthly fees may be higher than on longer contracts.

Mobile broadband contracts
With pay-monthly mobile broadband contracts, you must sign up to a direct debit agreement that takes a payment from your bank account on a monthly basis.

Some providers offer one-month contracts, which are fairly flexible. But you'll still have to sign up to a monthly direct debit and give notice of cancellation, so they're not quite as easy to change your mind about as a pay-as-you-go deal.

TRY THIS
If you will only use mobile broadband occasionally, then pay-as-you-go will be better for you. If you're likely to use it more often, such as during your daily commute to work, a pay-monthly contract is likely to be more cost-effective.

▶ Getting Online

If you're sure mobile broadband is right for you, you may get more for your money with a 12-, 18- or 24-month contract, since most contract tariffs include a free laptop dongle (see page 180 for more about dongles).

Bear in mind, though, that what's on offer in the mobile broadband world may change rapidly. If you sign up to a long contract, you won't be able to take advantage of any better deals that come onto the market, as contract cancellation fees can be steep.

Mobile phone internet connection

Some providers may offer a discount on mobile broadband if you also have a mobile phone service with them – ask about this when you sign up.

Accessing the mobile broadband network

Mobile broadband 3G coverage claims range from 80 per cent to 99 per cent depending on the provider – but quantity doesn't always equal quality, so impressive claims must be taken with a pinch of salt.

3G coverage is better in UK towns and cities – in more rural parts it can be patchy. However, in some rural areas you may be able to get mobile broadband access even if you can't get fixed-line broadband.

Mobile broadband availability

There have been cases of people taking out a mobile broadband contract only to discover that they can't get a signal in the locations they want to use it.

There are a few ways to reduce the risk of being tied in to a contract for a service you can't get:

▶ Check providers' 3G mobile coverage using the 3G maps or postcode checkers on their websites. But bear in mind that these are guides rather than guarantees to a service. You may also run into mobile broadband reception problems if you live in a location where mobile signals may be blocked by your surroundings, such as in a basement flat

▶ If you're concerned about getting a 3G mobile broadband signal, you could try borrowing a friend's 3G mobile phone to check that you can get a 3G mobile signal in your home. If you can get a mobile operator's

3G signal on your mobile phone, then mobile broadband from that mobile operator should also work at that location

▶ Before you buy, check the retailer's policy for allowing returns if you can't get a decent signal. Once you've bought a service, set up and check it as soon as possible after you get it home. That way, you'll hopefully find out if there's a problem with the signal in plenty of time to cancel for a full refund

If you want to get an overview of which providers are likely to offer the best 3G mobile coverage, check Ofcom's 3G maps at http://licensing.ofcom.org.uk/radiocommunication-licences/mobile-wireless-broadband/cellular/3g/maps/3gmaps/.

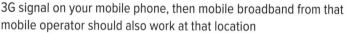

Mobile broadband speed

Maximum mobile broadband speed isn't as fast as traditional broadband yet – typically either up to 3.6Mbps or up to 7.2Mbps, though some mobile broadband speeds are a little slower.

You'll get the fastest speeds if you're on an HSDPA network. HSDPA stands for High-Speed Downlink Packet Access. It's sometimes also referred to as 3G+ or 3.5G. HSDPA is basically a faster form of 3G, meaning that your mobile broadband speed will be faster wherever there's an HSDPA/3G+ signal. HSDPA/3G+ coverage isn't quite as widespread as standard 3G, but both coverage and potential speeds are increasing.

Speed limitations

Mobile broadband has similar speed limitations to fixed-line broadband, meaning that the maximum speeds cited are a theoretical rather than a practical maximum. Distance from the nearest 3G mobile mast, plus additional factors such as physical obstacles (dense tree growth, for example) blocking the signal can all affect the actual broadband speed you'll get.

Even if you stand next to the mast, you won't be able to get the absolute maximum speed because of factors that limit speeds between the mast and the core network (known as 'backhaul').

Usage limits

Mobile broadband usage limits, or caps, restrict the amount of internet data, such as web pages and online video, that you can download or upload over your internet connection each month. Mobile broadband usage caps are fairly low – between 1GB to 3GB a month is typical – and some one-month or pay-as-you-go deals offer even less.

Many fixed-line broadband providers offer high caps or unlimited usage at a much lower cost.

Typical mobile broadband capped limits should be plenty for relatively light internet users – 3GB a month would let you to surf the web for six hours a day, send and receive 300 emails a week and download 90 music tracks a week.

If you exceed your mobile broadband usage limit, costs can be high. If you use the internet heavily – to watch online TV, play online gaming, or send and receive large files – you may be better off sticking to traditional broadband.

Using mobile broadband abroad

Technically, you can use mobile broadband overseas as long as there's a 3G mobile signal. But overseas mobile broadband usage won't be included in your fixed fee, and charges can be very high – usually several pounds per megabyte (MB), depending on your network and the country you're going to.

A single music track is around 4MB – so costs for using mobile broadband abroad can build up very quickly. There have been cases of people running up bills of thousands of pounds despite relatively restrained use. Be sceptical if a salesperson claims your usual monthly fee covers you to use your mobile broadband overseas.

Security issues

As with any internet service, security is paramount to avoid your laptop becoming infected with viruses and other internet nasties. You'll need a firewall, plus anti-virus, anti-spyware and anti-spam functions. (See page 56 for more information on laptop security.)

MOBILE BROADBAND ON YOUR LAPTOP

To access the mobile broadband network from your laptop, netbook or MacBook, you will need a mobile broadband dongle. Alternatively, you may have a laptop model with built-in 3G capabilities.

USB dongles

Most dongles are small USB receivers that look a bit like memory sticks. You just plug the dongle into one of your computer's USB ports and it will provide 3G mobile broadband service.

You can use a USB dongle in multiple computers, but you won't be able to connect more than one computer at a time unless you buy a separate mobile broadband wireless router. Ask your provider whether it offers mobile broadband routers, or you can buy one, such as the Billion BiPAC 7402GXL (from around £75).

Wireless dongles

Some mobile providers offer a more advanced type of dongle that allows you to connect multiple devices to the mobile internet wirelessly. Wireless dongles essentially give you your own portable mobile broadband Wi-Fi hotspot. One major advantage is that, unlike normal USB dongles, you can use mobile Wi-Fi to connect an iPhone or iPod Touch to the internet too.

Mobile broadband laptops

With some laptops you no longer need a dongle to get mobile broadband – the capability is built into the laptop itself. You're more likely to come across this if you take out a mobile broadband contract that includes a 'free' laptop in the monthly cost.

Going for a mobile broadband deal that includes a laptop can help you to spread the cost of a new computer, but in the long run it can work out more expensive than buying a laptop and mobile broadband separately.

If you're tempted by the convenience of a laptop with built-in mobile broadband, check with your chosen operator whether you'll be able to use the same laptop with a different provider when your initial contract comes to an end. If not, you won't have the option to switch to a network that may better serve your needs at that time.

Setting up mobile broadband on your laptop

Setting up mobile broadband on your laptop, netbook or MacBook is straightforward. Once you've agreed a mobile broadband contract, you will receive a free dongle modem (if your contract specifies this – alternatively you can buy a dongle from your ISP or other outlets). You will also receive a SIM card that contains all information needed to activate your account, along with an extension USB cable and user manual. The USB cable allows you to position the dongle away from your laptop in order to receive a stronger signal, especially in a location where physical obstructions block the signal.

1. Take the top off the USB dongle and insert the SIM card into the slot that's visible just underneath the connector. Push the SIM card completely into the slot, but don't force it.

2. Place the dongle into a USB port on your laptop. Most dongles come with all the necessary drivers for Windows and Mac OS so the connection software should launch automatically.

3. Follow the online instructions to complete the installation and start your online session.

4. The next time you plug in, you will be able to connect to the internet straightaway.

MOBILE BROADBAND ON OTHER DEVICES

You can get mobile broadband on your other devices such as:

Tablet PCs

Most tablet PCs offer Wi-Fi connectivity that makes accessing the internet easy via broadband networks at home and Wi-Fi hotspots when out and about. Some models also offer 3G connectivity (typically you will have to pay more for this hardware option) which means more freedom to connect to the internet through an ISP's mobile broadband network.

To connect to a mobile broadband network you need to purchase a microSIM card that you insert into the tablet, along with a payment plan from your chosen ISP. As with laptop dongles, there's a choice of PAYG and monthly contracts. Deciding on which one will depend on your usage and downloads – each plan will have limits which are expensive if exceeded.

Don't assume that the plan you purchase will cover connecting to the internet while travelling abroad with your tablet PC. Be sure to check with your ISP's terms and conditions to avoid very expensive bills.

Once you've purchased a mobile broadband payment plan, you will receive a microSIM card. Insert this into the relevant slot on your tablet PC or iPad, then follow the instructions on your device, or those supplied with the microSIM card.

Ebook readers

Several ebook readers offer built-in free 3G connectivity, although in the UK this is limited to Amazon's Kindle ebook readers.

Amazon's 3G connectivity, known as Whispernet, is limited to the Amazon Kindle store rather than full internet access. It does mean that you can use your Kindle anywhere (provided there is network coverage) to browse the Kindle store, purchase and download ebooks directly to your reader without having to plug it into a PC. See page 192 for How to set up wireless and 3G on a Kindle.

Smartphones

One of the benefits of a smartphone is the ability to get online wherever you are. A mobile internet connection is made over your mobile provider's network. As long as you have a mobile signal, you can access smartphone broadband to check email, surf the internet, or view or download files.

Capable of speeds up to 14.4Mbps, HSDPA technology currently offers the quickest connection speed, so if you plan on using mobile internet a lot, make sure your smartphone will support this type of connection.

Like standard mobile phones, smartphone payment deals are available as either a monthly contract, or PAYG. Use a free comparison website such as Which? Mobile (www.which.co.uk/mobile/) to choose the best payment plan for your smartphone.

If you want to make the most your smartphone's 3G internet capabilities, be sure to select a tariff that includes generous provision for data usage. Data usage limits how much you can download on your smartphone every month. If you exceed this allowance you may be subject to additional charges.

Monthly smartphone contracts typically offer the most free minutes, texts and data allowance included. This is offset by a longer contract period and higher monthly bills, which in turn is used to subsidise a free or cheap handset.

TRY THIS

Some web sites are available in special mobile versions and, if so, the URL will end in .mobi rather than .com or .co.uk. These versions have been optimised for fast download, and to be viewed on the smaller screens of smartphones and mobile phones with internet access.

GOING ONLINE USING WI-FI

Another way of connecting to the internet is by Wi-Fi (short for Wireless Fidelity) technology, which is wireless networking.

How Wi-Fi works

Wireless networking uses radio waves to transmit data to the internet or a home or office network – often known as local area network (LAN).

Most new laptops and mobile devices come with built-in wireless transmitters, which are a special kind of chip. If your laptop doesn't, you can buy a wireless adapter that plugs into the PC card slot or USB port.

Your laptop or mobile device uses its built-in Wi-Fi capabilities to convert data into the form of radio waves and transmits it to a router, through an antenna. The router decodes this information and transmits it to the internet via a physical ethernet connection.

Data from the internet follows the same path in reverse back to your laptop or mobile device.

How a Wi-Fi network works sounds complex, but to set one up you need two parts: a 'sender' and a 'receiver'. The 'sender' is typically a wireless router that includes a modem that connects to the internet. A 'receiver' is the special chip inside a laptop or mobile device that receives the data transmissions from the 'sender', or router.

As Wi-Fi involves a physical ethernet connection between the router and a modem, you're limited to using your laptop or mobile device at a set distance from a Wi-Fi router. Depending on the type of Wi-Fi your device and router uses, this is limited to around 50m (150ft).

As long as they all have wireless adapters, several devices can use one router to connect to the internet. This makes a wireless connection great for all your home computing, as all the Wi-Fi capable devices in your home can connect to a Wi-Fi router, then onto the internet. See page 189 for how to set up a wireless home network.

Wi-Fi speeds

Wireless networking is also referred to by its standard designation of 802.11. You will usually see this written with letters added after 802.11, which refer to the type of wireless network it is and the speed of data transfer it can achieve.

Many mobile devices use 802.11g, which supports a maximum bandwidth of 54Mbps. A newer standard known as 802.11n claims a maximum data rate of 248Mbps. 802.11n devices should also have a longer range than their predecessors, making them more efficient if, for example, you want to use your laptop at the bottom of the garden.

Security issues

Wireless Wi-Fi networks are great for the home. But, as devices don't need to be physically connected to a Wi-Fi router, and given the range a Wi-Fi router can transmit 50m (150ft) or more, devices outside your home can pick up your Wi-Fi signal, and potentially connect to it.

To ensure that your Wi-Fi network is safe, make sure that you set up and secure your Wi-Fi network (see page 191 for details on doing this).

It is especially important that you use a strong password that is a mix of characters, numbers and symbols. You can replace letters with symbols to make a memorable, but secure, password. For example, 'password' could be changed to 'p@ssw0rd' making it harder for devices to guess your Wi-Fi network password when attempting to connect to it.

USING WI-FI WHEN OUT AND ABOUT

A Wi-Fi hotspot is a public wireless access point, where you can connect to the internet at broadband speeds using your laptop or wireless-enabled smartphone or device. It is similar to using a wireless router at home.

Some Wi-Fi hotspots are free to use – usually those found in commercial premises such as coffee shops – but most require you to pay in some form. There's often a choice of payment method. If the hotspot is provided by a café you may pay for an hour of use, much as you would in an internet café.

If the Wi-Fi hotspot is provided by BT Openzone, T-Mobile or The Cloud, you can buy a voucher for the network that lasts an hour, a day or even a month.

If you want to use wireless hotspots regularly, subscribe to a package. These give you unlimited usage or a set number of minutes on a particular provider's hotspots every month, typically for £10 to £25 per month.

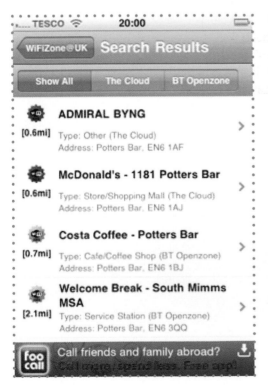

Finding hotspots

Each Wi-Fi provider has its own hotspot directory and finder, and there are many websites for finding Wi-Fi hotspots. These include:

- ▶ www.MyHotspots.co.uk
- ▶ www.JiWire.com, which provides a global Wi-Fi hotspot finder
- ▶ www.AtLarge.com, which provides reviews of UK and worldwide airport Wi-Fi services

You can also download free and paid-for apps that help you to find Wi-Fi networks for smartphones and mobiles, including the iPhone.

For example, the WiFiZone@UK app gives a free directory of BT Openzone, The Cloud, Orange and T-Mobile hotspots nearest to your current location, and can filter the list of Wi-Fi hotspots by operator.

WiFiTrak (59p) claims to give an improved Wi-Fi network finder compared to the built-in iPhone Wi-Fi function, and can be set to automatically scan and find networks that are in range.

Public Wi-Fi

Public Wi-Fi is available in a wide variety of locations, including:

▶ airport terminals and lounges
▶ pubs, bars, cafés and restaurants
▶ city centres and business parks
▶ clubs, schools, colleges and universities
▶ hotels, conference centres and exhibition halls
▶ railway stations, motorway service stations and shopping centres

City-wide Wi-Fi

Twelve UK city centres operate an urban mesh of wireless networks – on the BT Openzone network. These are: Glasgow, Edinburgh, Newcastle, Leeds, Liverpool, Sheffield, Nottingham, Birmingham, Cardiff, Bristol, Portsmouth, and Westminster and Waltham Forest in London.

Using Wi-Fi hotspots abroad

Some Wi-Fi hotspot operators have roaming agreements with international operators. For example, BT Openzone offers International Vouchers for 500 minutes of flat-rate web access (valid for 14 days) that can be used worldwide including the US, South Africa and Australia.

USING WI-FI ON YOUR MOBILE DEVICES

From laptops and netbooks to ebook readers and smartphones, many mobile devices now offer built-in Wi-Fi capabilities.

Wi-Fi on laptops and netbooks

Most laptops and netbooks have a built-in wireless transmitter that should automatically detect wireless networks within a certain range of your location. It will ask you if you wish to connect and allow you to select any of the existing networks.

Wi-Fi on a laptop is extremely convenient, as it gives you access to wireless internet, even outside your office or home.

Wi-Fi on tablet PCs

For connecting to the internet, most tablets offer built-in Wi-Fi connectivity for easy connection to broadband networks at home, and Wi-Fi hotspots when out and about. Wi-Fi networks will normally be detected automatically as soon as they come within range of the device.

Wi-Fi on ebook readers

Several manufacturers including Amazon Kindle, iRiver, and Samsung now offer ebook readers with Wi-Fi capability. This feature allows you to search, buy and download ebooks from an associated store directly to reader without having to be connected to your PC.

Amazon's Kindle DX has an experimental web browser that lets you surf the web over a Wi-Fi connection.

Wi-Fi on smartphones

Many smartphones now come with built-in Wi-Fi, which offers a great alternative to using your provider's phone network for surfing the Web. You can get a fast data transfer rate, which makes it easy to browse the internet or download files. Watching streaming movies and videos online is easy because of the no-lag connection. You can also make free calls from the internet through VoIP (Voice over Internet Protocol).

On the downside, using Wi-Fi may drain the smartphone battery faster than is normal, and finding a strong Wi-Fi connection when you are out and about can be difficult.

SET UP A HOME WIRELESS NETWORK

At the heart of any home wireless network is a router with a built-in modem. Get the router set up correctly, and it's easy to set up and secure your wireless network.

Set up your router

1 First, attach a microfilter to the main phone socket (where the phone line enters the house)

2 Now connect the router. All the cables you need should be included in the box with the router. Plug one end of the modem cable into the relevant microfilter socket. Plug the other end into the back of your router

3 Now connect your router's power supply and switch it on

Connect your router to your laptop

1 The easiest way to set up your router is to first connect it to your laptop via an ethernet cable (which should be in the router box). Put one end into the ethernet socket on the laptop, the other into one of the four identical sockets on the router – it doesn't matter which

2 Start up your laptop. To configure the router, open your web browser. Enter the address of your router into the browser's address bar. This is a number listed in your router manual. Press **Enter**

3 You will then be asked for login details. The default username and password will be in your router manual

Change your settings

You'll see the router set-up page – it looks like a web page, from here you can make changes to the router.

1 To change the default password, click the **Administration** tab, enter a password in the password window, confirm it and **Save**

Jargon buster

Microfilter
A device that attaches to your telephone socket and allows you to make voice calls and use broadband at the same time.

⏵ Getting Online

Jargon buster ⏵

ADSL router
ADSL stands for Asymmetric Digital Subscriber Line. It is a copper wire telephone line that allows you to send information to other computers with the same ADSL system. A router is a device that allows the computers to connect to each other.

2 For the router to connect to the internet, you need to configure the ADSL part with the correct settings. To do this, click on the **Setup** tab

3 The router will ask you for your internet service provider user name and password, which will have been provided by the ISP. You may also be asked to enter details about 'encapsulation' or 'multiplexing'. If this happens, ask your ISP about what you should do

4 Scroll down and save your changes. You should now be able to connect to the internet on the laptop

Change setting to wireless

1 Click the **Wireless** tab in the router set-up page

2 Change the name of your network in the **Network Name (SSID)** field to something memorable, such as 'Home wireless'

3 Select **WPA-Personal** from the drop-down menu, and enter a pass phrase. This works like a password when you need to connect a device to the wireless network (make it memorable but not too obvious)

4 Click **Save** and unplug your ethernet cable

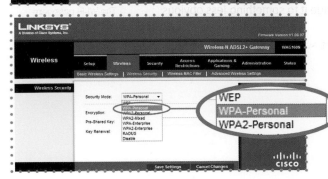

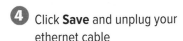

5 Your laptop should automatically detect wireless networks within its range. Yours will show up under the name you gave it in Step 2. Select it from the list, and connect to it. You'll be prompted for your security pass phrase – this is the same one you entered in Step 3

190

Secure your wireless network

Wireless networks bring with them certain security risks. As wireless-enabled devices will search automatically for any networks within range, and then connect to any that are open to them, it's vital to keep your network secure by taking these steps:

▶ All wireless networks have a name (sometimes called the SSID – see page 190) that you can change when you set up your router. Make it something that doesn't give any clues to your identity, or to the type of router that you're using

▶ If you're not planning to connect new devices to your network, consider turning off the router's broadcast network name (SSID). This will make it difficult for anyone looking for a network to connect to it

getting online

Jargon buster

SSID
The service set identifier is a way of naming a wireless network so it can be distinguished from others that are within range of a wirelessly-enabled device.

▶ Many routers come with weak passwords such as 'admin', which are easy for other people to guess. Change it to something less obvious

▶ Encrypt your network to make it more secure. Your router manual should show you how

TRY THIS

The Wi-Fi password information (or network key) is sometimes found on the physical router itself (often on the base) or in the documentation provided with the router.

▶ Getting Online

SET UP WI-FI AND 3G ON A KINDLE

The latest generation of Kindle ebook readers use both Wi-Fi and 3G to provide fast download and delivery of your ebooks and other content direct to your reader. The Kindle Wi-Fi ebook reader connects to the internet using public or private Wi-Fi networks, while the Kindle 3G includes both 3G and Wi-Fi connectivity, switching between either network to provide the best connection.

Join a Wi-Fi network on your Kindle

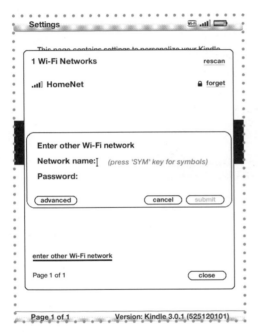

1 Press **Home** and then **Menu**. From the Menu options, choose **Settings**. Select **View** next to **Wi-Fi Settings**. This shows a list of available networks. If a network requires a password to enter, a lock symbol is displayed next to **Connect**

2 Select **Connect** to join a network. If prompted, enter the network password and click **Submit**

3 Once you have joined a Wi-Fi network, Kindle will automatically connect to it whenever that network is in range. If more than one previously joined network is in range, Kindle selects the one most recently used

4 Having connected to a Wi-Fi network, you'll see a Wi-Fi indicator at the top right corner of the screen

TRY THIS

To manually enter the network information for a Wi-Fi network, navigate to Enter other Wi-Fi network, as in step 5. Then choose **advanced** and enter the required network information, then select **connect** and the Kindle will connect to the new network.

5 To join a Wi-Fi network that isn't listed, select **Enter other Wi-Fi network**. Enter the network name and, if required, the password and select **Submit**

Kindle 3G (Whispernet)

If your Kindle is equipped with 3G, you will have access to Amazon's free 3G wireless called Whispernet, which uses Vodafone's mobile network.

This will be automatically available, though you will need to ensure that your Kindle is turned on for wireless. To do this, press the **Menu** button and select **Turn on Wireless**.

SYNCHRONISE YOUR DEVICES

With many people now owning a number of mobile devices – from smartphones and tablets, to ebook readers and laptops – it's useful to be able to synchronise (sync) information, files and data across devices.

This means that when you update information, such as create a new calendar event on a smartphone, or bookmark a page on an ebook reader, your other devices are automatically updated with that information. This means you can use any device at any time to access, change and update information and files, and all your other devices will reflect that change.

Syncing email, calendars and notes
Applies to: Laptops, tablets, smartphones.

The best way to synchronise email, calendars and notes is to use a free web service from Google, Yahoo or Microsoft.

How it works: On a laptop or desktop PC, use your web browser to create an online webmail, calendar and notes account with a company such as Google (see page 167 for a step-by-step guide). Any email, notes or calendar events created are stored on the servers of that company – and you simply enter the password and user account name of that service on devices such as smartphones and tablets.

Whenever you receive or send an email from one device, the online account stores the information. When accessed by a further device, you'll gain instant access to the latest events, emails and notes you have created on any of the devices connected to the account.

Syncing social networks
Applies to: Laptops, tablets, smartphones, some ebook readers.

Social networks, such as Twitter, LinkedIn and Facebook, allow you to tell groups of friends what you're doing and upload and share photos and video for others to view.

▶ Getting Online

How it works: Social networking sites can be accessed on a laptop using a web browser. On mobile devices, such as smartphones and tablets, you'll need to download a specific application from, for example, Apple's App Store, that gives access to your social networking service, such as Facebook or LinkedIn. Any changes you make on one device are instantly available across all devices.

Syncing music, video and photos
Applies to: Laptops, smartphones and tablet PCs.

Smartphones and tablet PCs can sync photos, music and videos with a laptop or desktop PC. This means that you can transfer your photos from a laptop to a tablet, or easily copy photos taken with a smartphone to a laptop, for example.

How it works (iOS - iPhone and iPad): Apple uses its iTunes as a digital hub for music, videos and photos. You connect the iPad or iPhone to your laptop and manage your media files from there.

How it works (Android smartphones and tablets): Like the iPhone and iPad, you'll need to physically connect your Android-based smartphone or tablet to a laptop. It uses software such as Windows Media Player to synchronise files including audio. Alternatively, most Android devices can be mounted onto the desktop PC in much the same way as a removable hard drive, allowing media files to be dragged and dropped on to the device.

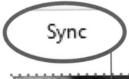

Syncing files
Applies to: Laptops, smartphones and tablets.

There are lots of ways to synchronise files – such as Microsoft Word documents – between devices to ensure that you are always working on the most up-to-date version.

How it works (iOS – iPhone and iPad): Apple uses iTunes to synchronise a limited range of files, such as Microsoft Word files. Connect your iPad (see page 103 for details) or iPhone, then choose Apps from the device tab. Check the applications and documents you wish to synchronise.

How it works (Android-based devices): Each Android device can either be mounted as a hard drive onto a laptop, use an online storage service such as Dropbox (see page 158), or use a dedicated desktop software client to handle file transfer. For example, the Samsung Galaxy Tab uses the software Samsung Kies on a laptop to sync files when the tablet is connected to the PC using a USB cable.

Alternatively, for both Android and iOS devices, third-party storage services, such as Dropbox, can be downloaded as apps on to the mobile device. This gives you access to online storage where you save your documents. Any device accessing your Dropbox account can view, edit, save and sync documents.

Syncing ebooks

Applies to: Laptops, ebook readers, smartphones, tablets.

Ebook syncing allows you to read an ebook on one device – such as a tablet – then continue reading from the last page you were at on another device, automatically. You can also synchronise margin notes, annotations and bookmarks on supported devices.

How it works: All devices – from the Amazon Kindle to the Apple iPad – use their own system for handling the synchronisation, but the process is similar across them all. Your mobile device needs to be linked to your account (such as your Amazon or iTunes account), and connected to the internet via 3G mobile broadband or Wi-Fi. With the account active, other devices connected to the same account will automatically sync to the last read page when you use the device, without you having to do anything.

▶ Getting Online

WATCH OUT!
Remote media streaming is available only in the Home Premium, Professional, Ultimate, and Enterprise editions of Windows 7.

SHARING MEDIA ACROSS DEVICES

In Windows 7, you can create a Homegroup network to share media and document files across any device that's connected to that network (see page 51).

Windows 7 offers media streaming (see page 188) with Windows Media Player 12's **Play To** feature. This makes it easy to send music, photos, and videos from one computer to another, or any compatible media device such as a stereo or TV, that's connected to your Homegroup. For example, you can view your photos from the computer in your spare bedroom or study, on a digital picture frame or laptop in your living room.

Furthermore, with Windows 7's remote media streaming, you can enjoy the music, videos, and pictures on your home desktop PC while you're away. Remote streaming only works on two computers running Windows 7, and you will need to set up remote media streaming on both computers first, but after that when you're next on the road, your home PC media library will automatically appear in Windows Media Player on your laptop.

Get started with streaming
To stream your media at home, you need the following hardware:

▶ A wired or wireless private network
▶ Either a second computer on your network, or a device known as a digital media receiver. For example, this could be a suitably equipped television

Turn on streaming

 Click **Start, All Programs**, then click **Windows Media Player**

2 Click **Stream**, and then click **Turn on home media streaming**

3 On the Media streaming options page, click **Turn on media streaming**

4 Click **OK**

Changing settings

You can choose what to stream, and create different rules for each computer or device that receives streams on your network. You can, for example, choose not to stream music with explicit lyrics or pictures rated less than two star.

1 Click more **Media Streaming options**

2 Click **Customize**

3 Untick the box next to **Use default settings**. Then set the options under star and parental rating as you wish

4 Click **OK**

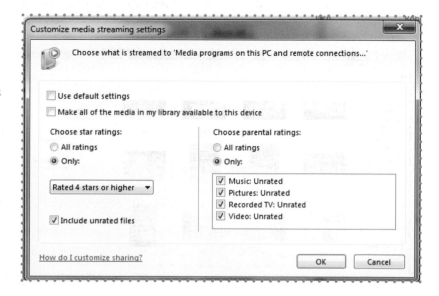

▶ Getting Online

Stream media using Play To in Windows Media Player
Windows Media Player 12's Play To feature lets you stream music, videos, and pictures to other computers and devices on your home network so you can enjoy them whichever room you are in.

1 First, in Windows Media Player, make sure **Turn on home media streaming** is ticked under the **Stream** menu

2 Click the **Play** tab

3 Find the items that you want to play in the Player Library, and then drag those items from the details pane into the list pane

4 Click the **Play to** button at the top of the list pane, and then click the device on your network that will receive the streamed media

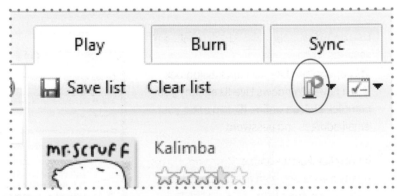

5 In the **Play To** dialog box, use the controls to play, pause, or stop the media stream, and to change to the next or previous item in the list

Remote media streaming

To use remote media streaming, both computers (for example a home desktop PC and a laptop) need to be running Windows 7.

You also need an online ID for secure access to your home computer over the internet. By linking this online ID, such as a Windows Live account, with a Windows user account, your home computer will allow access from a remote laptop or computer that has the same online ID.

1 Open Windows Media Player and click **Stream** in the upper-left corner of Windows Media Player

2 Click **Allow Internet access to home media**

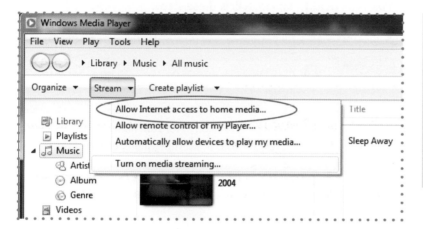

TRY THIS

If you have an online ID, such as a Windows Live account, for accessing email and instant messaging you can link this to a user account on your Windows 7 computer. Once linked, you can access files and stream media files on your home computer, over the internet.

3 In the next dialog box click **Link an online ID**

4 This opens the User Accounts dialog box. If you have a Windows Live ID already you can click **Link an online ID** and enter your email address and password

If not, click **Add an online ID provider.** This opens a webpage with a list of providers. Choose **Windows Live**, click the link to download, and click through the set-up assistant. Then go back to **User Accounts** dialog box, where you will see a Windows Live entry with a **Link an online ID** link

199

5 Click **OK**

6 Click **Allow Internet access to home media**

7 Repeat the set-up process on your laptop using the same online ID and you're ready to start streaming

Accessing your home media remotely

Once you've allowed internet access to home media, you're ready to play files remotely. The computer streaming the media must be connected to your home network and the PC or laptop receiving the stream must be connected to the internet.

On the remote PC or laptop, follow these steps:

1 Click **Start**, click **All Programs**, and then click **Windows Media Player**

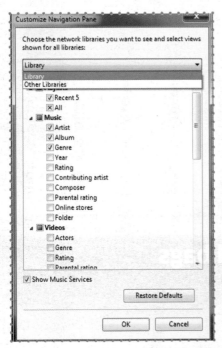

2 Click **Library** button in the upper-right corner of the Player

3 Find the Player Library for your home computer under **Other Libraries** in the navigation pane, and click it

4 You can now search for a file you want to play in the Player Library, and then double-click it.

If Other Libraries isn't available in the navigation pane, do the following:

1 Click **Organize**, and then click **Customize navigation**

2 At the top of this dialog box, click the name of the Library in the drop-down list, and then click **Other Libraries**

3 Select the **Show Other Libraries** check box, and then click **OK**

4 You can now search for a file you want to play in the Player Library, and then double-click it.

PROTECTION

By reading and following all the steps in this chapter, you will get to grips with:

Your buying rights

Keeping your device safe and avoiding theft

Choosing cases and bags

Protection

TRY THIS
The Which? website reviews hundreds of laptops, tablet PCs, ebook readers and smartphones. Check out www.which.co.uk

MOBILE DEVICES BUYING ADVICE

Always buy a brand you know and trust

Do some research, read trusted online and magazine reviews, or ask for recommendations from friends or colleagues.

Always pay for your purchase using a credit card

If you pay for goods that cost more than £100 using a credit card, the card company will take joint liability with the retailer if something goes wrong.

The Consumer Credit Act 1974 gives you extra protection if something you buy is faulty, not what your ordered, or doesn't turn up. It will even help to cover the cost of accidental damage before you get it home.

Know your rights

When you buy goods, such as mobile devices, you enter into a contract with the seller. Under the Sale of Goods Act 1979 the goods must be:

▶ 'as described',
▶ 'of satisfactory quality', and
▶ 'fit for purpose' – both their everyday purpose, and any purpose you agreed with the seller (for example, a printer compatible with a laptop)

Goods sold must also match any sample you were shown in the store, or any description in a brochure.

In most cases, your rights are against the retailer not the manufacturer, and so you must make any claim against the retailer. If a product turns out to be faulty, you can 'reject' it: return it and get your money back. The law gives you a 'reasonable' time to do this. This depends on the product and how obvious the fault is – usually no more than three to four weeks.

You have the right to get a faulty item replaced or repaired, if you're happy with this (or it's too late to reject it). You can ask the retailer to do either, but they can choose to do whatever would be cheapest.

Under the Sale of Goods Act, the retailer must repair or replace the goods 'within a reasonable time but without causing significant inconvenience'. If the seller doesn't do this, you are entitled to claim either:

▶ a reduction on the purchase price, or
▶ your money back, less a sum for the use you've had (called 'recision')

If the retailer refuses to repair the item, you may have the right to arrange for someone else to repair it, and then claim compensation from the retailer for the cost of doing this.

You have six years to make a claim for faulty goods in England, Wales and Northern Ireland; in Scotland you have five years.

Shopping online

Shopping online can be more convenient and cheaper than the high street, but it can be easy to make a mistake when ordering online, and sometimes what you receive isn't what you expected.

The good news is that if you buy online from a UK or EU-based retailer you've the same rights as if you'd bought from a shop. Furthermore, under the E-Commerce Regulations, online shops must set out the stages you have to complete before you place an order. You must also be given the chance to check your details before confirming the order. If the online shop confirms acceptance of your order, you have a legally binding contract, but, if it simply acknowledges your order, you don't.

The E-Commerce Regulations also state that the online shop has to give full details of who they are and provide a geographical address and an email address at which to contact them. The online shop's terms and conditions should also say who pays for returning goods. If they don't, then they have to pay.

Cooling-off period

If you change your mind about the items you've bought online, or they don't arrive on time, the Distance Selling Regulations (DSR) give you a cooling-off period. This starts from the moment you place the order and ends seven working days from the day after you receive the goods. During this period you can cancel without having to give a reason. Simply contact the retailer to get a refund and arrange a return of the goods.

Warranty issues

You may be offered the chance to buy an extended warranty when you purchase a laptop or mobile device.

First check the standard warranty that covers the item you want to buy. The manufacturer's standard warranty for goods such as laptops usually lasts for one year, although some may offer two or even three years.

TRY THIS

Always read the terms and conditions of your warranty before signing so you know exactly what is and isn't covered.

NEXT STEP

Buying an extended warranty that is backed by an insurance company gives you more rights if things go wrong.

▶ Protection

WATCH OUT!
Laptop batteries typically have a limited warranty, as performance depends on how they have been maintained.

If the basic warranty is only for a year, many retailers offer an extended warranty. Before you opt for this, it's worth considering the total cost of the item and additional warranty. If you're buying a budget laptop it may not be worth spending more to cover the cost of repair, if it costs nearly as much as buying a new computer. However, if you have purchased a more expensive laptop as a desktop replacement, you may prefer the security of knowing it can be repaired under an extended warranty.

If your new laptop is essential for work it may even be worth looking into onsite warranties, as this means an engineer will come to you, rather than you sending your laptop away to be repaired. These warranties are more expensive but may include extras such as a free replacement laptop should yours need to be returned to the manufacturer for a full repair.

TRY THIS
It's worth keeping the original packaging your laptop or mobile device came in, in case you need to return it to the manufacturer for repair.

Before you do buy an extended warranty, check the average turnaround time for repairs and who will be actually handle any repairs. Some companies will send your laptop away for repair – possibly back to the manufacturer – leading to a lengthy wait. Other companies will repair it there and then in the store. Also check if repairs under warranty will be guaranteed and for how long.

Warranty terms explained
Collect and return (C&R)
This means your mobile device would be collected, repaired and returned to you at no cost.

Return to base (RTB)
The repair is paid by the warranty, but you pay for the cost of arranging the transport of the product to be fixed.

Onsite warranty
The warranty supplier will arrange an engineer to visit you to repair the mobile device – but this is a costly warranty mainly used by businesses.

Global warranty
Some multi-national companies offer worldwide cover for mobile products, so you can get it repaired if it breaks down while you are travelling. Check the small print, as this will either mean taking it to an authorised repair centre, or it being fixed onsite.

PROTECT YOUR MOBILE DEVICES

Because of their portability, mobile devices and laptops are more prone to damage and theft than home-computing devices. Levels of theft of mobile devices are particularly high as they are small, easy to sell on, and have a relatively high value. If your device is stolen, not only are you out of pocket for the cost of the hardware, but for the applications you've purchased, and you have lost your files, such as photos and videos.

Tips for protecting your mobile device
Never leave your laptop or mobile device unattended
It only takes a minute for a thief to strike. If you work in an office, don't leave it on your desk – keep in a pocket, bag or lockable desk drawer.

Never leave a laptop or mobile device on display in a car
Thieves look for cars where valuables have been left on display. If you have to leave a device in a car, cover it or lock it in the boot.

When carrying a laptop, use an inconspicuous bag
Purpose-built cases make it obvious you're carrying expensive equipment. A rucksack or handbag makes you less likely to be targeted by thieves.

Mark your property
Use an ultraviolet pen to make a distinctive mark, or some other form of identification such as postcode and door number, on the device.

Register your mobile devices
Register your devices for free at Immobilise (www.immobolise.com), a list of ownership details that appear on the British police's property database.

Note down serial numbers
Make a note of the serial number, make and model of the laptop or mobile device and keep the information safe.

▶ Protection

TRY THIS

With most mobile phones, you can check the IMEI number by pressing * # 0 6 # on the phone keypad. The number will appear onscreen. Apple iPhones users can also find this number under Settings > General > About. The IMEI number is also usually printed inside the battery compartment of mobile phones.

With smartphones, note the IMEI (International Mobile Equipment Identity) number. This 15-digit code is a unique identifier for the phone. If it is stolen, the number helps your mobile service provider to block it.

Use a password

Passwords provide basic protection of personal information on all your mobile devices. Use your smartphone's security lock (PIN code) if it has one.

Back up your data

Back up the data on your laptop or mobile devices regularly and store the disks or drives somewhere safe at home.

If it's stolen

Report a stolen or lost device to the police immediately, followed by your ISP. The ISP can block a smartphone handset so that even if the SIM card is changed, it will not work in the UK. If you are insured, contact the insurer within 24 hours (most terms and conditions insist on this).

Insurance

Many companies offer polices for mobiles and devices. However, you may be covered by your home insurance policy. Laptops are often classed as high-risk items, so make sure you're covered, especially when travelling. If lost, a device should replaced with one of similar or better specification.

ENCRYPT INFORMATION ON YOUR LAPTOP

If you need to protect the information on your laptop from prying eyes, the ultimate way is to encrypt the data. You can encrypt the whole hard drive, or specific files and folders, using a variety of paid-for software.

Windows 7 Professional users can protect files or folders on their laptops using Windows Encrypting File System (EFS). This encrypts and decrypts files, providing an additional layer of security. The first time you encrypt a folder or file with EFS, an encryption file certificate is created. This is the key (or algorithm) used to encrypt a file. It is linked to the user account that encrypted the file or folder, so only that user can decrypt it.

Encrypt a file or folder in Windows 7 Professional

1 Log on to your laptop using your user account name and password

2 Right-click the folder or file you want to encrypt, then click **Properties**

❸ Click the **General** tab, and then click **Advanced**

❹ Select the **Encrypt contents to secure data** check box, click **OK**, then click **OK** again

Decrypt a file or folder in Windows 7 Professional

❶ Make sure you're logged on to your laptop using the same user account name and password as when you encrypted files previously.

❷ Right-click the folder or file you want to decrypt, then click **Properties**

❸ Click the **General** tab, and then click **Advanced**

❹ Unclick **Clear the Encrypt contents to secure data** check box, click **OK**, and then click **OK** again

Jargon buster

Encryption
The process of transforming data using a mathematical algorithm to make it unreadable to unauthorised readers.

It's important to back up encryption file certificates. If the certificate is lost or damaged, you won't be able to use the encrypted files.

Back up your encryption file certificate

❶ Click **Start** and then **Control Panel**

❷ Click on **User Accounts and Family Safety** then click **User Accounts**

❸ Click on **Manage your file Encryption Certificates**

❹ In the Encrypting File System wizard, click **Next**

❺ Click **Use this certificate**, and then click **Next**

❻ Click **Back up the certificate and key now**

❼ Select the location where you want to store the backup. A CD, USB flash drive or external hard drive are best

❽ Type and confirm a password for the backup file, then click **Next**

❾ Tick the **I'll update my encrypted files later check box**, then click **Next**

protection

ACCESSORIES FOR YOUR MOBILE DEVICE

Once you've bought your laptop or mobile device, it's wise to think about protecting it when you're out and about. There's a vast range of different options available for each type of mobile device, including sleeves (also called covers or skins), cases, bags, screen protectors and other accessories.

Laptops

Many laptop owners find that they need both a sleeve and a case for their laptops.

Sleeves

A good sleeve will protect your laptop from scratches and slight knocks, as well as from dirt and dust. There are lots of sleeves to choose from in a range of materials from soft fabric or neoprene covers, to hard materials such as leather or vinyl.

Make sure the sleeve you choose fits snugly around your laptop by choosing the correct size – most will come in a range of sizes to suit the many different types of laptops sold. Alternatively, look for a soft neoprene sleeve that will stretch around your laptop. Ensure that the sleeve closes securely with a velcro flap or zip, as this will stop the laptop from sliding out.

Bags and cases

As with sleeves, there's a huge choice when it comes to buying a purpose-built case. Styles include backpacks, briefcases and messenger bags, as well as handbag-styles designed for women.

If you plan to travel regularly with your laptop, you will need to consider security, protection and comfort, as well as personal style. Weight is another factor to keep in mind when looking at laptop bags.

Whatever style of bag you chose, look for one that is well-padded and has a secure means of strapping the laptop in place. Adjustable shoulder straps and plenty of storage space for small accessories are good features to have.

Tablet PCs

As with laptops, there's a vast choice of cases available for each type of tablet PC, from the practical to handmade or custom-designed cases that provide the chance to express your own personal style and individuality.

Cases and sleeves

Before choosing a case, consider how you will use your tablet PC. If it will be used mainly at home a good-value, soft sleeve will be fine, but if you plan to travel with it, look for something more durable and robust that protects the large screen.

Tablet cases are either similar to the soft laptop-style sleeve, or are a rigid hard shell material.

Soft sleeves – usually made from fabric or neoprene – provide a good basic pocket to slip your tablet PC in and out of quickly. Some even have windows through which to view your screen.

⊳ Protection

Hard, shell-like cases offer good protection and the material used in these include carbon and silicon. Hard cases usually snap on around the back of the tablet and cover the edges to protect against damage if dropped.

Other styles in hard material include book jacket style cases. These are suitable if you need something lightweight and slim to carry your tablet inside another bag.

Another popular style of case for tablets is the flip stand. This type offers a thin outer cover that folds out to prop up your tablet at various reading angles so you use the tablet without having to hold it.

Ebook readers

If your ebook reader doesn't come with a wallet or case, buying a separate case is worthwhile. As well as providing extra protection for your device, helping to prevent screen scratches, a wallet can also make the reader easier to hold, and feel more like a traditional book.

There are hundreds of ebook reader covers to choose from. You will find different sizes for different products, made from all kinds of materials, and some even come with useful extras. It's down to personal preference

which cover is best for you, but with so many to choose from, you're bound to find the perfect ebook reader cover for your taste and budget.

Some of the most popular material options for covers include:

Silicone covers provide simple protection for your ebook reader and the thinness of the material avoids adding bulk.

Leather covers usually open out like a book's front cover. More solid than the silicone cover, they protect the screen when you are carrying the reader. Although they are stylish, they do add bulk to your ebook reader.

Plastic covers work in a similar way to leather cases, but are a cheaper option. Plastic covers are available in a wide range of sizes and colours.

Special covers can be made from many types of material, but they usually include additional features such as moveable reading lights or pockets for storing paper or notes. Some also come with stands, enabling you to place your ebook reader upright on a table to read more easily.

Smartphones

If you've bought an expensive smartphone, spending some extra money on a case is a very wise precaution. Smartphones are generally more vulnerable to bumps and scratches than regular phones, especially if they have a large touchscreen, and they can be expensive to replace.

There are many differing varieties of cases. Bumpers, which are essentially rubber coatings for your phone, are a common mobile phone accessory, especially for smartphones. You can usually use the phone while it is in this form of case. You will have to remove it from many other styles of case.

Socks are simply a fabric sheath for your smartphone, and serve mainly to reduce the possibility of scratches and damage while the handset is in a handbag or pocket.

Cases often come in a flip design, and cover the front and back of the phone, protecting against damage.

Screen protectors are thin, transparent covers that you stick on top of the smartphone's screen to protect from scratches. Cheap to buy, they offer effective protection, particularly for touchscreen handsets that have large displays vulnerable to damage. It's sensible to buy these in large quantities, as some only last as little as a week before they lose their stickiness.

Finding the right case is as much about ergonomics as functionality. Matt rubber and silicon are good materials to have as a case, for example, as they reduce the chance of your smartphone slipping out of your hand.

Other useful mobile phone cases and holders

A belt clip case may be worth investing in if you're looking for something that makes your phone as accessible as possible. Similarly, a neoprene armband will allow you to hold your phone safely while you're running or at the gym.

Additional accessories for mobile devices

Beyond cases and bags, there are loads of accessories available for your mobile device. These range from headphones, wireless keyboards, speakers, stylus pens for smartphones and tablets to travel adaptors and in-car chargers. Make sure you read reviews of products or chat to friends to see which accessories they recommend.

RESOURCES

▶ Jargon Buster

2G Second generation – the name given to a group of the first digital mobile phone networks that were rolled out in the early 1990s. In the UK, most voice calls and texts are transmitted over a 2G GSM network.

3G The third generation of mobile networks, which allows large amounts of data to be sent wirelessly. Mobile broadband operates over the 3G network.

4G Fourth generation networks. These are the networks that will supersede 3G networks over the next few years. 4G networks will enable even faster broadband internet speeds on mobile phones.

ADSL (Asymmetric digital subscriber line) A way of sending data over a copper wire telephone line.

AMOLED (Active-matrix Light Emitting Diode) is a type of screen display technology used on high-end mobile phones. Super AMOLED is a variation of this technology, which allows for even brighter displays.

Anti-spyware Software that prevents and/or removes spyware.

Anti-virus Software that scans for viruses and removes them from your computer.

App Short for application software. Most apps are downloaded directly to a mobile device from an online store. They broaden the functionality of a smartphone or mobile device and essentially work in the same way as PC applications such as Microsoft Office, or Photoshop.

Bandwidth The maximum amount of information that can be transmitted across a connection; usually measured in megabits per second.

Bluetooth A type of wireless technology that allows information to be transferred from one device to another, over relatively short distances. Commonly used by smartphones, and to transfer data from mobile devices to computers.

Boot time The time it takes for a computer to start working from switching it on.

Broadband A method of connecting to the internet via cable or ADSL. Much faster than a dial-up connection.

Cashback A special deal offered by mobile phone retailers. The customer can claim back some of the cost of a smartphone contract over a certain period of time.

Computer interface The programming code that allows software, such as applications, to talk to the computer hardware. It also is used to describe the appearance of screen menus and the controls you use to interact with the computer.

CPU (Central Processing Unit) Often just called the processor, it is the nerve centre of a computer. The best-known PC processors are Intel's Pentium and AMD's Athlon.

Crash When a computer program or operating system stops working completely, or almost completely, it is said to have 'crashed'. When a computer crashes it usually needs to be restarted (also referred to as re-booted) before it can be used again.

DDR (Double Data Rate) A fast type of Ram for PCs, originally for high performance graphics cards, now used for general memory in high-end PCs. DDR2 is even faster.

Desktop A computer designed to sit on a desk (as opposed to a laptop). In operating systems such as Windows, it also means the screen you see when you aren't running any programs, with 'My Computer', the Recycle Bin and so on.

Dial-up Internet connection via a telephone line; slow compared with broadband.

Dongle A small device that connects to a computer's USB port. In this context, it enables you to connect to the internet.

Download To transfer data from a remote computer to your own over the internet.

Driver Software that allows your computer to communicate with other devices such as a printer.

Digital Rights Management (DRM) A system for protecting the copyright of digital content (such as music, books, images and video) that is distributed online, whether it is downloaded, printed or viewed or shared across computers and other devices.

EDGE (Enhanced Data Rates for GSM Evolution) A 2.5G network technology. EDGE was developed to allow 2G GSM networks to connect users to the internet more effectively. Although it is faster than GSM connections, EDGE is much slower than 3G networks such as UMTS.

Email client A computer program that manages emails. Emails are stored on your computer, and you only need connect to the internet to send and receive emails.

Encryption The process of transforming data using a mathematical algorithm to make it unreadable to unauthorized readers.

Ethernet A means of connecting computers together using cables – a common method for networking computers.

External hard drive A storage device that plugs into your PC. Useful for saving copies of important files or creating additional storage.

Firewall Software (or hardware) that blocks unwanted communication from, and often to, the internet.

FireWire Fast connection suitable for transferring large amounts of data, such as video footage, from devices. FireWire cables plug into a FireWire port.

Frequency band Mobile phones transmit data over radio waves and this is the radio frequency a phone uses. Different countries use different bands. Some phones support just two frequencies, while others support three and four, enabling you to use your phone across different networks in different countries.

FTP (File Transfer Protocol) Ability to transfer rapidly entire files from one computer to another, intact for viewing or other purposes.

GB (Gigabyte) A measurement of data. 1GB equals one thousand megabytes (MB). Often used by mobile phone operators to measure data usage on internet tariffs.

GPS (Global Positioning System) A form of technology that allows the location of your mobile device to be tracked by a satellite. This information can then be used in conjunction with navigational apps, such as Google Maps.

▶ Jargon Buster

GSM (Global System for Mobile Communications) The mobile phone network technology standard that is used in the UK. It is the 2nd generation (2G) network standard that nearly all voice calls and texts are transmitted over.

HD (High Definition) A format that allows visual content, such as video, to be displayed at a very high resolution.

HDMI (High Definition Multimedia Interface) a digital connection that can transfer uncompressed high-definition video and audio to your television or monitor.

HSDPA (High-Speed Downlink Packet Access) A type of 3G network protocol (sometimes dubbed 3.5G) employed on UMTS networks.

Hyperlink Text or image that, when clicked, allows you jump to another web page when surfing the internet; in the case of ebooks, takes you to another, linked page.

ISP (Internet service provider) The company that enables and services your connection to the internet.

LCD (Liquid Crystal Display) Liquid crystal cells change reflectivity when an electric current is applied to produce slim, bright but low-power screen displays.

Malware Short for malicious software, this is software developed for the purpose of causing harm to a computer system.

MB (Megabyte) A measurement of data, 1MB equals one thousand kilobytes (KB). Commonly used to describe disk storage and data transmission rates.

Mbps (Megabits per second) A measure of the speed of data transfer, often used when talking about the speed of broadband.

Memory card A removable storage device, available in a variety of sizes and formats including SD card, Smart Media, CompactFlash, and Sony Memory Stick.

Memory stick A small portable device used to store and transfer data. It plugs into a USB port and is also called a USB key, flash drive or pen drive.

Microfilter A device that attaches to your telephone socket and enables you to make voice calls and use broadband at the same time via ADSL.

MicroSD A removable data storage format that can hold all types of files, such as MP3s, documents, pictures and video. Due to their small size, MicroSD cards can be frequently found in mobile phones.

MMS (Multimedia Message Service) An extension of SMS, which lets users send multimedia content, such as pictures and videos, between mobile phones.

Modem A device that allows a computer to send information over a telephone line. You need a modem to connect to the internet.

Mp (megapixel) The unit of measurement used to represent the size and resolution of a digital image. One megapixel is equal to one million pixels.

Motherboard The circuit board that houses the laptop's CPU, memory slots, video chip, and other essential components of a computer.